POPE PIUS XII: NOT GUILTY!

Pope Pius XII: Not Guilty!

Douglas Sczygelski

Published by Douglas Sczygelski, 2016.

POPE PIUS XII: NOT GUILTY!

First edition. May 5, 2016.

ISBN: 979-8231721320

Written by Douglas Sczygelski.

Table of Contents

To my family, from whom I learned so much.

INTRODUCTION

Why did Pope Pius XII not publicly denounce the Holocaust while it was going on?

The answer is that he did, though not often, and not vehemently.

There seems to have been only one time when someone pressed him to explain his policy. One German bishop, Konrad von Preysing, wrote repeatedly to Pius during the war, asking him to speak out more forcefully. Pius eventually wrote back and said he thought public condemnations wouldn't do much good, and would provoke severe reprisals by Hitler against Catholics. (Endnote 1.) Of course, Pius's critics think that was nothing but a flimsy excuse and couldn't possibly have been his real reason.

So let's analyze the question.

ITEM 1: THE JUDGMENT OF SAUL FRIEDLANDER

Saul Friedlander is a history professor at UCLA, one of the world's leading experts on the Holocaust, and author of a massive book about the Holocaust called *The Years of Extermination: Nazi Germany and the Jews, 1939-1945*, which won a Pulitzer Prize. Friedlander is Jewish, and as a boy he barely managed to escape the Holocaust himself. He has looked into the question of Pius's behavior during the Holocaust and has concluded that, of course, nobody can read Pius's mind, but it is certainly possible that Pius sincerely believed that public criticism would accomplish little or nothing useful, and sincerely believed that Hitler would retaliate by killing a large number of gentile Catholics, by ordering his thugs to arrest and kill Catholic Jews and Catholic half-Jews in Italy and elsewhere, and by thoroughly searching convents, monasteries and churches in Italy for Jews who were being hidden there by priests and nuns. In Friedlander's words, "hundreds, perhaps thousands" of Jews were hidden in Italian churches, convents and monasteries during the war. (Endnote 2.) Friedlander believes that it was reasonable for Pius to draw those conclusions. There is nothing Pius did, in Friedlander's opinion, that was so irrational that one can say it must have been motivated by antisemitism.

Friedlander has also concluded that in Hungary, the Catholic archbishop and the Protestant leaders were able to protect the Christian Jews precisely because they refrained from complaining when the other Jews were rounded up and sent to death camps. (Endnote 3.)

Daniel J. Goldhagen, Pius's most vehement critic, responds to this theory with silence. On page 54 of his book, *A Moral Reckoning*, he insists that there is no reason to believe the pope's silence saved anyone, but he fails to discuss the idea that Hitler would've responded to criticism by killing Catholic gentiles, by killing Catholic Jews and Catholic half-Jews, and by searching Italian convents, monasteries and churches for hidden Jews. Apparently Goldhagen cannot bear to even consider that possibility.

On page 50 of his book, *A Moral Reckoning*, Goldhagen discusses the time when the Nazis in the Netherlands started arresting Jews and sending them to concentration camps. The Catholic and Protestant bishops told the Nazi governor that they would publicly condemn this action if it didn't stop. The Nazi governor replied that if they publicly condemned it, he would retaliate by arresting all the Catholic and Protestant Jews in the Netherlands. In the face of this threat, the Protestant bishops backed down, but the Catholic bishops went ahead with their public statement, and in retaliation, all the Catholic Jews in the Netherlands were arrested and killed. Goldhagen says this incident proves nothing, because the Protestant Jews were eventually arrested and killed even though the Dutch Protestant bishops kept silent. However, he is missing the point. One would think, logically, that Nazi policy would've been the same everywhere in Europe, but it is a simple historical fact that in some countries, Christian Jews were arrested and killed, and in others they were left alone. Because of the uncertainty about whether Nazi policy might change at any moment, it was perfectly reasonable for Pius to be afraid that if he made this or that statement, the Nazis might retaliate against the Catholic Jews and Catholic half-Jews of Italy and/or other countries. Is Goldhagen really going to sit there and say he is absolutely certain that Pius should not have been afraid of that? Is Goldhagen really going to say he is absolutely certain that public condemnations by the pope would not have provoked some grisly retaliation by Hitler? I don't see how any sensible person could feel certain about such a thing.

One must keep in mind that between September 1939 and June 1941, the Nazis murdered approximately 20 percent of the Catholic priests in the part of Poland that they ruled. It would've been easy for the Nazis to raise that percentage. When Pius sent a letter to Hitler complaining about Nazi brutality in Poland, the Nazi foreign minister replied by threatening to make the situation worse if Pius publicly complained. (Endnote 4.)

Thousands of Catholic priests, nuns, and Protestant pastors were arrested in Germany by Hitler, even before the war began. Does Goldhagen have any theory about why that happened? Has he not, at least, heard of the famous Lutheran clergyman Martin Niemoller, who spent eight years in the Dachau concentration camp and was freed only when the war ended? In May 1936, Niemoller and some of his friends sent Hitler a letter, demanding an end to government interference in their churches. Hitler responded to this by arresting hundreds of Niemoller's followers and confiscating their organization's money. (Endnote 5.) Is Goldhagen going to be honest enough to admit that Hitler did that because he wouldn't tolerate even the slightest criticism?

Has Goldhagen, at least, heard of Sophie Scholl and her friends, seven college students who formed a group called the White Rose, and who were arrested and killed just because they handed out a few anti-Nazi pamphlets in 1942? (Endnote 6.) Doesn't that prove that criticizing Hitler was a dangerous activity?

Has Goldhagen ever heard of Anna Rosmus? She was a teenager in West Germany when she became curious to know what had happened in her town during the war. This annoyed many people who preferred to cover up the past, and she became the target of considerable harassment. A movie called *The Nasty Girl* was based on her travails. In an interview once, she mentioned, "A priest was murdered for defending the Jews in church. Another priest refused to swear an oath of loyalty to Hitler. He was killed too. But nobody ever spoke about these men with any respect. They had broken the rules." (Endnote 7.)

But Goldhagen sits there and insists there was no danger that Hitler would seek revenge when he was criticized.

Goldhagen talks about a Catholic bishop named Clemens von Galen who publicly denounced Hitler's policy of exterminating the severely mentally ill. Galen was not punished for this, and Goldhagen thinks that means that German Catholic and Protestant bishops could have publicly denounced the Holocaust at no risk to themselves. First, let me point out that Galen's denunciations did not accomplish much. The killings continued, though in greater secrecy. (Endnote 8.) Second, let me point out that Hitler told his assistants that Galen would be executed eventually, after the war was won. (Endnote 9.) Third, isn't it common knowledge that exterminating the Jews was a cause nearer and dearer to Hitler's heart than exterminating the mentally ill? Hitler considered the Jews a deadly threat to Germany, but considered the severely mentally ill to be merely a nuisance and a burden.

On page 55 of *A Moral Reckoning*, Goldhagen says a public condemnation of the Holocaust by the pope would have severely hampered Hitler's plans, but we can see in the above quote from Anna Rosmus that when some clergymen tried to stand up to Hitler, the common people did not support them. Shirer saw that too, when he was living in Germany. As he phrased it, "Not many Germans lost much sleep over the arrests of a few thousand pastors, priests and nuns." (Endnote 10.) If the German people weren't moved to action when they saw German pastors, priests and nuns being carted off to prison, why would they be moved to action by the persecution of Jews? In 1943, the German Catholic bishops published a public letter saying that one must respect the right to life of all people, even "human beings of alien races and origin." (Endnote 11.) This public statement seems to have had no impact whatever. Pius also, in his Christmas address on Vatican radio in 1942, denounced the idea that governments have the right to "herd people around as though they were a lifeless thing," and lamented that currently in Europe there were "hundreds of thousands of persons who, without any fault on their part, sometimes only because of their nationality or race, have been consigned to death or to a slow decline." (Endnote 12.) That, too, seems to have had no impact on the people who were carrying out Hitler's plans.

On page 307 of *A Moral Reckoning*, Goldhagen mentions a Protestant town in France called Le Chambon, where the townspeople saved three thousand Jews by hiding them from the Nazis. Goldhagen says every Catholic priest in Hitler's empire could have and should have acted that way. Unfortunately for Goldhagen, after he wrote *A Moral Reckoning*, more research was done into what actually happened at Le Chambon, and it was discovered that Le Chambon was able to hide its Jews because "the village was in fact being protected by a Gestapo official, who gave the mayor prior warning of raids, and by sympathetic elements in the local Vichy police." (Endnote 13.) Therefore, Goldhagen's claim that Catholic priests throughout Europe could have done what the people of Le Chambon did is obviously not true. The people of Le Chambon were in a very unusual situation. Goldhagen also fails to see that if such actions had been more common, the Nazi efforts to stamp them out would have surely been more vigorous. In Poland, the penalty for helping Jews was death. (Endnote 14.) That wasn't automatically the penalty anywhere else in Hitler's empire, but surely the Nazis could have made it so. Doesn't Goldhagen know that Victor Kugler, the Dutchman who hid Anne Frank and her family, was arrested and sent to a slave labor camp? (Endnote 15.) Kugler lucked out, in the end. One day, when he and some other prisoners were being marched from one place to another, an Allied fighter plane strafed them. In the confusion, Kugler escaped.

Let us look at what Friedlander says: helping Jews "entailed risk, extreme risk in Eastern Europe, various degrees of risk in the West." (Endnote 16.) Goldhagen should admit that.

Getting rid of the Jews was Hitler's main goal in life. Difficult though this may be to believe, winning the war came second. That is why Hitler preferred to kill Jews rather than use them for slave labor. Anyone who knows the history of World War One knows that most of the Jews in Germany and Austria-Hungary supported the war effort, some quite enthusiastically. Even Sigmund Freud openly supported the Austro-Hungarian war effort, as you can see in any scholarly biography of the man. Look, especially, at Fritz Haber, a scientific genius who won the Nobel Prize in chemistry and spent World War One running munitions factories and poison gas factories for the kaiser. I think it is safe to say that no one person did more to help the German war effort in World War One than Haber, and he did this despite the fact that there was quite a bit of discrimination against Jews in Germany in those days. Yet, when Hitler came to power, he considered Haber just another Jew, and Haber had to flee Germany for his life. (There is an article about Haber in Wikipedia.) I think it is safe to say that most of the Jews in Hitler's empire would've been perfectly willing to help Hitler win the war, if only Hitler had let them do so and had treated them at least semi-decently, and Hitler's chances of winning the war would have been greatly improved if he had had his thugs spend more time at the front and less time arresting and killing Jews.

But no, killing Jews was Hitler's obsession. He would've taken extreme measures to punish anyone who interfered with that goal. When a high-ranking Nazi named Reinhard Heydrich was assassinated by Czech resistance fighters in 1942, Hitler retaliated by murdering 340 Czechs in the village of Lidice. (Endnote 17.) He also murdered approximately a million Polish gentile civilians. (Endnote 18.) It is easy to imagine that he would have killed a hundred thousand more Polish, Czech, Dutch, Belgian and French Catholic civilians in retaliation if Pius had harshly criticized him. For some reason, Pius's critics are never willing to discuss this.

ITEM 2: PIUS XII NEVER ORDERED ANYONE TO DO ANYTHING DANGEROUS

Widespread efforts by Catholic laymen, priests and nuns to hide Jews, similar to what the people of Le Chambon did, surely would have gotten large numbers of Catholics killed. Surely it would also have saved some Jewish lives. A large number of Jewish lives, or just a small number? I suspect it would've been a small number, though of course I can't prove that.

One has to remember that there were food shortages throughout Hitler's empire during the war, and food was rationed, so even if you were brave enough to hide some Jews, how on Earth were you going to feed them? A Dutch lady named Corrie Ten Boom hid some Jews in her house, and was arrested for it and sent to a concentration camp, and became famous after the war by writing a book about her experiences, but she had a friend in the food-rationing office who gave her extra ration coupons. (Endnote 19.) Obviously, not everybody had a friend like that.

(One of the little-known facts of the war is that President Roosevelt, with the support of Congress and America's military leaders, wanted to send food to the starving people in Hitler's empire, but Winston Churchill adamantly opposed any such plan, saying it would indirectly help Hitler. Roosevelt backed down in the face of Churchill's bluster, so in the end, only small amounts of food were sent. There is no doubt that food shortages raised the death rate among civilians in Hitler's empire, because people weakened by malnutrition died of diseases that ordinarily would not have killed them. Endnote 20.)

But the simple fact is that Pius never ordered people to take actions that carried a significant risk of death. Let me repeat that for emphasis, because it is too often overlooked: Pius, in his entire life, never ordered people to do things that carried a significant risk of death. I defy anyone to name a time when he did. For example, after the war, even though he detested communism and greatly feared that Stalin was planning to start World War Three, he never ordered young Catholic men who lived in communist countries to dodge the draft, because he was afraid, with good reason, that they would be killed for that. He certainly never ordered Catholics in communist countries to revolt against the government, or to hinder communist armies in any way. You can call that a cowardly policy if you like, but he stuck to it consistently throughout his reign.

I'm old enough to remember the Cold War. One never heard American liberals or socialists say the pope should order young Catholic men in the communist countries to dodge the draft. Does Goldhagen seriously think that is what the Cold War popes should have done?

ITEM 3: PIUS XII AND STALIN

Friedlander, as I said above, believes Pius may have sincerely believed that public condemnation would provoke Hitler to kill Catholic gentiles, and kill Catholic Jews and Catholic half-Jews, and to thoroughly search Italian convents, monasteries, and churches for Jews who had been hidden there. But Friedlander also believes Pius's actions were guided mainly neither by hatred for Jews nor by concern for them, but by his fear of Stalin. Pius feared that victory for the Americans, British and Soviets would mean that Stalin would grab a big chunk of eastern and central Europe, including many Catholic countries. Then, Pius feared, Stalin would murder millions of people in eastern and central Europe, just as he had in the Soviet Union in the 1930s. Pius hoped he could keep Stalin out of eastern and central Europe by somehow engineering a peace deal between the Nazis, the British and the Americans that would allow the Nazis to go on fighting the Soviet Union. (Endnote 21.) Then, he apparently hoped that Hitler would be overthrown by his generals or succeeded eventually by someone more reasonable. Look at the way Pius tried to assist a group of German military officers who were plotting to overthrow Hitler early in the war. (Endnote 22.) Look at the way the Vatican's official newspaper, during the war, said repeatedly that Pius was willing to mediate peace talks. (Endnote 23.) The British ambassador to the Vatican also believed that Pius was refraining from harsh condemnations of either side because he hoped he would be able to mediate peace talks. (Endnote 24.)

To keep this hope alive, Pius decided that he couldn't afford to offend Hitler, so he kept his public criticisms rare and not very specific.

Was Pius wrong to think that way? It seems to me that it was perfectly reasonable for him to conclude that Stalin was worse than Hitler, given the information that he had at the time. Now days we think of Hitler as the epitome of evil, and it is true that in the long run, Hitler murdered more people than Stalin, but Stalin did his murdering first. In the early 1930s, Stalin confiscated the grain of the peasants of the Ukraine and other places, causing more than 5 million people to die of starvation. (Endnote 25.) Then, in 1937-1938, Stalin had his Great Terror, which killed about 700,000 more. (Endnote 26.) Hitler, prior to the day he invaded Poland, had murdered only about ten thousand people (Endnote 27) therefore, prior to the day he invaded Poland, it was perfectly logical to prefer being ruled by Hitler to being ruled by Stalin.

(But some people think Snyder's estimate of the number of people killed by Stalin is too low. When Gorbachev ruled the Soviet Union, he asked his assistant Alexander Yakovlev to examine the records and figure out how many people Stalin murdered. Yakovlev came up with an estimate of 15 million, which is slightly more than the number Snyder thinks Hitler killed. Endnote 28.)

It is also worth remembering that during the Spanish Civil War, which lasted from 1936 to 1939, the Spanish leftists murdered 6,832 Catholic priests and 283 nuns. (Endnote 29.) There wasn't one speck of evidence that any of them had committed a crime. Surely that had some impact on Pius's thinking. He may have thought that Stalin, if he ever got the chance, would do something similar in the Catholic countries of eastern Europe.

Goldhagen, however, on page 88 of his book *A Moral Reckoning*, says he cannot understand why Pope Pius XI in 1937 denounced communism much more harshly than he denounced Nazism. Boy oh boy, he just can't understand it. Is Goldhagen really so ignorant that he is unaware of the fact that as of 1937, Stalin had already murdered millions while Hitler had murdered only a few thousand? Did it never occur to him to ask?

Even when Hitler started committing mass murder, it was not immediately clear that he would outdo Stalin. In fact, if we believe Yakovlev's estimate, he never did.

Look at this astounding fact: after Stalin grabbed eastern Poland and the Baltic states, "thousands" of Jews fled Stalin's empire to live instead in Hitler's empire. (Endnote 30.) It sounds like some kind of stupid joke, but it's true. Thousands of Jews sized up the situation in 1940 and decided they would be more likely to survive under Hitler than under Stalin, because Stalin seemed to have a policy of killing anybody who had been a successful businessman.

Of course, in the end, Stalin did not commit mass murder in eastern Europe on the same scale as he had in the Soviet Union in the 1930s. He had many Germans, both soldiers and civilians, arrested in the last months of the war and in the first post-war months, and sent them to slave-labor camps in the Soviet Union. Six hundred thousand of them died in those camps. (Endnote 31.) But ghastly though that was, it was not on the same level as the carnage that he had created in the Soviet Union. One wonders why. Perhaps he had simply decided that mass murder was not a good idea, that there were better methods for holding onto power. Or perhaps he would've killed millions in eastern Europe if he had lived longer. At the time of his death, there were signs that he was planning a massive new purge. (Endnote 32.)

But in any event, there was no way for Pius to know, during the war, that Soviet rule in eastern Europe would not be as harsh as it was in the Soviet Union. Logically, he had to assume that it would be about the same.

ITEM 4: HITLER'S RETALIATION

Friedlander is not alone in thinking that Pius was motivated by a desire to forge an anti-Soviet alliance. Michael Phayer, too, has reached that conclusion. In addition, Phayer believes Pius was worried that if he denounced Hitler, Hitler would retaliate by bombing the city of Rome into a smoldering ruin. Phayer thinks Pius wanted to avoid that, both to prevent Romans from being killed, and because he feared the faith of Catholics all over the world would be shaken if the city of Rome was demolished. (Endnote 33.) This makes Pius's refusal to complain when a thousand Roman Jews were arrested more comprehensible. Some people have asked why Pius didn't just go to the train station where those Jews were being loaded and demand that the loading stop. Apparently, part of the answer is that he was afraid that if he did that, and the loading stopped, Hitler would have killed those Jews by ordering his military to simply demolish the entire city.

That incident is worth examining. On October, 16, 1943, the Germans arrested approximately a thousand Jews in Rome, and were obviously planning to kill them all. In response, the Vatican secretary of state, Cardinal Luigi Maglione, summoned the German ambassador for a talk. He vaguely threatened that if those Jews were sent to a death camp, the pope would publicly complain. The German ambassador responded by threatening that there would be "consequences" if the pope did that. There were about 6,700 Jews in hiding in church-owned buildings in Rome and the vicinity, and the ambassador vaguely hinted that the Germans might intensify their searches for those hidden Jews. (Endnote 34.)

So, Pius decided to say nothing when the one thousand Jews were deported and killed.

Goldhagen seems to think it is obvious that Pius made the wrong choice. I don't think that is obvious at all.

ITEM 5: HIGH-LEVEL MISTAKES

Even if one believes it was stupid for Pius to be so afraid of retaliation from Hitler, one must admit, stupid decisions by major leaders have been common in the twentieth and twenty-first centuries. Wasn't the Bay of Pigs fiasco a stupid blunder by President Kennedy? Wasn't it stupid for President Reagan and Secretary of State George Shultz to get the United States involved in Lebanon? Wasn't it stupid for Tsar Nicholas II to declare in 1914 that he was going to support the Serbs, come what may? Wasn't it stupid in 1956 for the British and French to think they could get away with seizing the Suez Canal from Egypt? Wasn't it stupid for Neville Chamberlain to betray Czechoslovakia? Wasn't it stupid for the French to waste so much money and so many soldiers' lives trying to hold onto Vietnam and Algeria? Wasn't it idiotic for Jimmy Carter to approve that bizarre hostage rescue operation in April 1980? (Colin Powell says on page 249 of his autobiography that the plan was "foolhardy" and that if he had been asked to evaluate it in advance, he would've said the chance of success was around one percent.) Many conservatives say it was idiotic for Lyndon Johnson to refuse to bomb Hanoi and the supply ships that were arriving every day in Haiphong harbor. (Endnote 35.) Liberals, on the other hand, think it was stupid for Lyndon Johnson to fight in Vietnam at all. If those stupid decisions weren't caused by antisemitism, why should we assume a stupid decision (if that is what it was) by Pius XII was caused by antisemitism?

If you want to see real stupidity, look at an opinion piece that George Orwell wrote in October 1938, when Hitler was demanding that he be given the Sudetenland. Believe it or not, Orwell said all sensible Britons should oppose going to war against Hitler to defend Czechoslovakia, because what Britain needed was a socialist revolution, not a war. (Endnote 36.) People such as Orwell and Neville Chamberlain simply could not see that alliances, such as the one between Britain, France, and Czechoslovakia, were essential to the defense of freedom. Winston Churchill saw in 1938 that abandoning Czechoslovakia would be both immoral and stupid. He told Chamberlain, after Chamberlain betrayed Czechoslovakia, "You had a choice between war and dishonor. You chose dishonor and you will have war." Those words ring down through the ages. But few in Britain agreed with Churchill at the time.

Then in July 1939, Orwell wrote another essay, called "Not Counting Niggers," in which he declared that there wasn't a dime's worth of difference between Hitler and the British ruling class. Britain and France both were running huge empires full of low-paid natives who were hardly better off than slaves, Orwell said, therefore Britain and France were not worth defending. What British blue-collar workers really needed, he said, was not an anti-fascist war against Germany and Italy but "a real mass party whose first pledges are to refuse war and right imperial injustice." (Endnote 37.)

Keep in mind that Orwell wrote that even after Hitler had made it clear that his favorite method for handling critics was to have them dragged out of their beds in the middle of the night and shot, and even after the *Kristallnacht*, that night in November 1938 when howling mobs of Nazis all over Germany burned synagogues, looted Jewish shops, and lynched scores of Jews in the streets. That, Orwell said, was no worse than the behavior of the British government. How could he have been so stupid? Did he not see that if Hitler conquered the British and French empires, the lives of the natives in the colonies would only have gotten worse? Hitler would've simply shot Gandhi and all the other Indian nationalists, and he would've treated the blacks in Africa like dogs.

(In August 1939, Orwell suddenly changed his mind, and he supported the British war effort all through the war. You can read about that in any good biography of Orwell.)

Let's also look at the thoughts of Bertrand Russell, the famous British libertine and philosophy professor who, for years, was a sort of pope of atheism in the English-speaking world. In 1936, he wrote a book called *Which Way to Peace?* in which he said that modern war was so hideously destructive that if Hitler attacked Britain and France, the British and French should just surrender to him. (Endnote 38.) (Can you imagine how the militant atheists would be screaming today if any pope had ever said anything like that?) In March 1939, Russell wrote that if Britain and Germany went to war against each other, the United States should stay neutral and do absolutely nothing to help the British. He even said that if war came, pacifists in Britain should refuse to care for wounded soldiers. (Endnote 39.)

Isn't it interesting that one never hears militant atheists denouncing Bertrand Russell for giving aid and comfort to Hitler for years? They'll complain all day about Pius XII, but they ignore what the atheist Russell did.

Is Goldhagen going to argue that Orwell and Russell made those statements because they were antisemitic? Of course not. Orwell and Russell just made huge mistakes. If Orwell and Russell could make huge mistakes, what is so strange about the idea that Pius might have made one too?

ITEM 6: THE PROBLEM OF FAIRNESS

Another possible explanation: Pius told an American diplomat during the war that if he publicly condemned Hitler's atrocities, he would have to publicly condemn Stalin's atrocities too in order to be fair, and that might've been bad for the Allies. It might've reduced the enthusiasm of many Americans, Britons and Frenchmen for the war effort. (Endnote 40.) Nowhere in his book does Goldhagen consider that possibility.

One must remember, Pius never condemned the Allied bombing of civilians in Germany either. The famous firebombing of Dresden was passed over in silence by the Vatican. Not even Goldhagen claims otherwise. Pius was evenhanded. He condemned no one publicly, except when he made rather vague public complaints about Hitler's actions.

ITEM 7: THE TRAGEDY OF POLAND

If you are going to say that Pius's vague complaints about the Holocaust proved he didn't care about the Jews, then you must ask, did his silence about Poland mean he didn't care about Poles? It is a simple fact, though little-known in the United States, that Hitler murdered approximately a million Polish gentiles, and that 600,000 more Polish gentiles were killed while fighting against Hitler. (Endnote 41.) The pope complained about this in public, but not often, and not vehemently. Phayer describes what happened. In 1939, the pope issued an encyclical called *Summi Pontificatus* in which he lamented the horrible sufferings of the Polish people, but he did not condemn Germany and did not point out that the sufferings of the Polish people were being caused by the Germans. (Endnote 42.) Oddly enough, he didn't condemn the Soviets for invading Poland either, even though he detested communism. Next, in January 1940, a Vatican radio broadcast complained that both Jews and gentiles were being terrorized by the Germans in Poland and faced "starvation" because the Germans had confiscated so much of Poland's food supply. (Endnote 43.) In November 1940, another Vatican radio broadcast said things in Poland hadn't gotten any better. (Endnote 44.) On May 31, 1943, Pius talked about the terrible sufferings of the Polish people, and two days later, on June 2, he gave a speech to a group of cardinals and again lamented the suffering in Poland, but in neither of those speeches did he criticize Germany or point out that Poland's suffering was being caused by Germany. (Endnote 45.) And that is the total record of Pius's statements about Poland during World War Two. It is startling to see that in October 1941, the Vatican's official newspaper reported the death of a Polish bishop, Leon Wetmanski, without mentioning that he died in Auschwitz. (Endnote 46.) As I said earlier, Pius sometimes complained to Hitler through diplomatic channels about Nazi atrocities in Poland, but the only response he ever got was a warning from the Nazi foreign minister to shut up or else things would become worse. (Endnote 47.) Hitler himself, in a conversation with an Italian diplomat that was reported to Pius, raged that he would demolish the Vatican if Pius complained publicly about his policies in Poland. (Endnote 48.)

Many Poles were quite upset about Pius's policy of silence. Bishop Karol Radonski summarized the situation in Poland by saying that, "hundreds of priests are dead or imprisoned, nuns are in the hands of spoiled depraved thieves, innocent hostages are murdered almost daily before the eyes of children, people are dying of hunger, and the pope keeps silent as if what happens to his flock doesn't concern him." (Endnote 49.) One can't help noticing how similar that sounds to Goldhagen's statements about Pius and the Jews.

The Polish ambassador to the Vatican made sure Pius was kept informed about events. He reports that one day in 1944 Pius said at the start of a meeting with him, "I have listened again and again to your representations about our unhappy children in Poland. Must I be given the same story yet again?" (Endnote 50.)

So what does Goldhagen say about Pius's response to German atrocities in Poland? Nothing. He mentions that Pius complained about Hitler's treatment of the Poles, but he fails to mention that Pius's complaints had no impact and were insignificant compared to the enormity of the atrocities that Hitler committed against Polish gentiles. The fact that approximately 1.6 million Polish gentiles were killed by Hitler seems to simply escape Goldhagen's notice. It shouldn't. This question cannot be evaded: why did Pius not order German Catholics to do everything they could to help the Poles? Why did he not excommunicate every German who took part in military operations in Poland? Did he simply hate Poland? No expert believes that. Instead, you are left with the idea that I discussed in Item 3:

that Pius believed that to save Europe as a whole from the nightmare of Stalinism, he needed to try to build an alliance between Britain, France, the United States and Germany, and that this meant he had to avoid getting Hitler too angry at him, and that therefore he couldn't complain much about Hitler's behavior in Poland. He pleaded with Hitler through diplomatic channels to show the Poles some mercy, but he hurled no public thunderbolts of condemnation. He thought he had to sacrifice Poland to save Europe as a whole. He saw no good alternative. And this also explains why he said so little about the Holocaust.

But Goldhagen refuses to admit that, or to even discuss the theory. If he did, he would have to admit that it all makes sense.

(Of course, as I have already said, Pius also said once in a letter to a bishop that he believed vehement public condemnations would not do much good, and would cause Hitler to retaliate by murdering large numbers of Catholics in Poland and perhaps other countries as well. (Endnote 51.) And, as I have also already said, the Nazi foreign minister sent a letter to Pius one day, threatening retaliation if Pius publicly condemned Hitler's policies. Endnote 52.)

It is true that Pius never used diplomatic channels to urge Hitler to ease up on the Jews, but it is impossible to believe that such a message would've had any impact anyway, and perhaps Pius was thinking that first he would try to get Hitler to ease up on the Poles, and then, if that worked, he would move on to stage two: trying to get Hitler to ease up on the Jews. But Hitler never eased up on the Poles, at least not by much, so Pius never made it to stage two.

ITEM 8: THE CATHOLIC VICTIMS

Let us also remember that on June 30, 1934, when Hitler carried out his famous "Blood Purge," four of the victims, executed without a trial and without having committed any crime, were prominent Catholic laypeople: Erich Klausener, the head of Catholic Action, an organization of laypeople that was dedicated to doing just about anything the German bishops thought needed to be done; Adalbert Probst, the leader of the Catholic sports association; Fritz Gerlich, former editor of a Catholic newspaper, *Der Gerade Weg* and a frequent critic of the Nazis; and Fritz Beck, the leader of a Catholic college student association. (Endnote 53.) To add insult to injury, Hitler had them cremated, which was forbidden by church law in those days. (Endnote 54.) The German bishops and Pope Pius XI uttered not one word of protest against these murders. Lewy concludes that they were simply afraid that if they started an all-out struggle against Hitler, the laypeople would not back them up, and the church would be wiped out. (Endnote 55.)

What would Goldhagen say about that? He thinks Pius XII said nothing when Jews were murdered because he felt contempt for Jews. Does he also think Pius XI said nothing when Klausener, Probst, Beck and Gerlich were murdered because he felt contempt for them? That would be absurd. Klausener, Probst, Beck and Gerlich were the most loyal sons the church could ask for. But Goldhagen says absolutely nothing about the murders of those four men, because that incident proves that the pope and the German bishops sincerely believed that loud protests against Hitler's atrocities would only make things worse. Goldhagen ignores the whole issue. He is too cowardly to face a tough question.

Let us also look at the fact that on July 25, 1934, some Austrian Nazis assassinated the Austrian dictator, a Catholic named Engelbert Dollfuss. Nobody has ever proved that Hitler ordered the murder of

Dollfuss, but no historian seriously doubts it either. It is undeniable that he was glad when he heard the news. Someone who was with him at the time has written, "he could scarcely wipe the delight from his face." (Endnote 56.) Pope Pius XI, on the other hand, was depressed by the news. He believed democracy inevitably led to rule by demagogues such as Hitler and Mussolini, so a Catholic dictator such as Dollfuss was exactly the kind of man he liked seeing at the head of nations. (Endnote 57.) So why did Pius XI not condemn Hitler for killing Dollfus? One has to assume that he thought a public condemnation would do more harm than good. What other reason could there be?

Hitler also outlawed all Catholic lay organizations, such as the Catholic Young Men's Association. Instead, he made membership in the Hitler Youth compulsory, even though Hitler Youth meetings contained what the German Catholic bishops considered anti-Christian propaganda. The bishops complained, but always backed down in the end. Then Hitler outlawed all Catholic daily newspapers, and some of the Catholic weeklies too. The remaining Catholic weeklies had to submit to censorship. (Endnote 58.)

Somehow, Goldhagen never finds time to mention all that. Why did the popes and the German Catholic bishops put up with such treatment? Because they thought they had no choice. They thought that if they started an all-out struggle against Hitler, they would lose and the church would be wiped out.

In 1934, *Der Sturmer*, the semi-official newspaper of the Nazi Party, printed a cartoon that depicted Jesus as a Jew, drinking a chalice of Christian blood. Some Christian clergymen sent Hitler a letter of complaint about this. Two weeks later, Hitler ordered that no more copies of that issue of *Der Sturmer* be printed or sold. (Endnote 59.) Of course, by then, everybody who wanted to buy a copy of that issue had already done so. This is the sort of stuff the Christian bishops of Germany put up with, because they thought publicly lambasting the Nazis over actions like this would only make the situation worse.

ITEM 9: ISRAEL AND GUATEMALA

Goldhagen is also the author of a rather dull book called *Worse than War: Genocide, Eliminationism, and the Ongoing Assault on Humanity.* On page 256, he complains that the United States assisted the Guatemalan government in the 1980s in murdering 200,000 Guatemalan peasants. On that page and elsewhere in the book he talks at great length about how evil the Guatemalan government was in those days. There was a rebellion in Guatemala at the time, and the government strategy was to kill anybody who seemed even slightly inclined to support the rebellion, in order to terrorize the peasants into submission. As a result, huge numbers of innocent civilians were killed.

For purposes of this e-pamphlet, I am not going to analyze the question of whether the Reagan administration's policy in Guatemala was morally justified. That is an argument for another day. All I am going to say is that Goldhagen's denunciations lead to a question. If Goldhagen is going to yell on and on about how awful it was that Pius's condemnations of the Holocaust were so rare and vague, why doesn't he say anything about the Israeli government and Guatemala? I don't think Israel has any special duty to care about human rights all over the world, but surely all human beings should care about human rights, so why didn't the Israeli ambassador to the United Nations give a speech denouncing the Guatemalan government and demanding economic sanctions, or even military intervention, to force Guatemala's rulers to behave decently? I know for fact that the Israeli government never did that, because the Israeli government sold weapons to the Guatemalan government, which were used to carry out the 200,000 killings that Goldhagen denounces. (Endnote 60.)

Let's give Goldhagen the benefit of the doubt and assume that he is unaware that Israel sold weapons to the Guatemalan generals who were committing mass murder. The fact remains that Goldhagen surely knows, or ought to know, that Israel's prime ministers during the

1980s, and many other world leaders as well, ignored the killings in Guatemala. That action, by itself, is slightly worse than Pius's behavior during the Holocaust. (At least Pius talked about the Holocaust a little bit.) If you are going to condemn Pius for saying so little during the Holocaust, you must also condemn the Israeli leaders in the 1980s. But Goldhagen doesn't do that. Neither in *A Moral Reckoning* nor in *Worse than War* does he criticize anything the Israeli leaders did, nor does he explain why he isn't criticizing them.

He who condemns Pius's silence sees nothing wrong with an Israeli prime minister's silence.

Of course, one might argue that Israel is so dependent on American good will that no Israeli prime minister would dare to say something that might arouse the ire of an American president, but if we accept that argument, then we also must accept the argument that Pius did not dare to criticize Hitler much for fear of his wrath.

And what about Rwanda? In 1994, during the genocide, did the Israeli prime minister offer to send Israeli troops to Rwanda as part of an international force to protect the Tutsis? Not that I ever heard. The Israeli prime minister wasn't going to risk his troops' lives just to save a bunch of Rwandans, and for that matter, Bill Clinton wouldn't either. Clinton wasn't going to risk the lives of Americans in order to save Rwandans, just as Pius refused to risk the lives of Catholics in order to save Jews. Goldhagen condemns Clinton for this, but do the liberals? A few do, but most do not. Clinton was re-nominated by the Democratic Party in 1996 without any difficulty. And what about Syria? Read pages 373 thru 377 of the book *The Education of an Idealist: A Memoir*, by Samantha Power, Obama's ambassador to the United Nations, and you will see that Power vehemently advocated using the American military to stop Bashar al-Assad from committing mass murder, but Obama rejected her advice. On page 330 of her book, *What Happened*, Hillary Clinton says that when she was secretary of state, she wanted Obama to establish "a no-fly zone in Syria," which of course would have carried the risk of American pilots being shot down. Obama responded to Clinton's advice by making the same decision that Pius made. Obama wasn't going to risk the lives of American troops to save a bunch of Syrians. Few liberals criticized him for this.

ITEM 10: THE SILENCE OF THE SCIENTISTS

Another way to look at it is this: if you wonder why Pius's denunciations of the Holocaust were not louder, angrier and more specific, then you should also wonder why Steven Weinberg, Murray Gell-Mann, Richard Feynman, Sheldon Glashow and other Nobel Prize-winning scientists did not denounce the policy of mass murder that, in their opinion, was carried out by the Reagan administration in El Salvador, Nicaragua and Guatemala in the 1980s.

(This is not the place to discuss the pros and cons of the Reagan administration's Central America policy. Here, I will point out only that American liberals certainly thought that policy was nothing but mass murder, and I take it for granted that prominent physics professors such as Weinberg, Gell-Mann, Feynman and Glashow agreed with that assessment. The fact that few professors at America's leading universities are conservatives is common knowledge, something that neither liberals nor conservatives deny.)

The pope has a lot of prestige, but Nobel Prize-winning scientists have a lot of prestige too. If forty American Nobel Prize-winning scientists had signed a petition saying Reagan was nothing but a murderer, and that his policy in Central America was no better than Mussolini's invasion of Ethiopia, that he ought to be sent to Nuremberg and put on trial for mass murder, maybe that would've started the process of turning the tide of public opinion against his Central America policy. If they had actually taken some time out of their busy lives to go to Washington and hold a press conference, that might've had even more impact. Or look at Carl Sagan. He was one of the most famous men in the United States in the 1980s. His political views were very liberal, perhaps even socialist, as any biography of him will show. He wrote many books, and he could've written one called *Reagan is Committing Mass Murder in El Salvador*. Nothing was stopping him. A book with such a provocative title would surely have made the bestsellers list. But that book never appeared. Why did Sagan, Weinberg, Feymann, Gell-Mann, and Glashow show so little interest in the sufferings of their fellow human beings?

Pius, at least, could plausibly argue that he was afraid that if he had made vehement anti-Hitler public statements, Hitler would've retaliated against the Church in some gruesome way. Weinberg, Gell-Mann, Sagan and the other scientists had no such excuse. They didn't have to worry about being arrested and tortured to death for criticizing Reagan.

And for that matter, look at all the other celebrities who did nothing. Jimmy Carter could've run around the country calling Reagan a murderer, driving from college campus to college campus, paying for the trip by passing the hat at each lecture. It would not have cost him much. In every town, I'm sure he would've found plenty of Democrats willing to let him spend the night in their homes, free of charge. Ted Kennedy, with his enormous fortune, could have done that too. After Jerry Brown's second term as governor of California ended in 1983, what was stopping him from doing that? What was stopping Walter Cronkite, Bill Moyers, George McGovern, and Barbara Walters? After Cronkite retired, he could've written a book called *Reagan is Committing Mass Murder in El Salvador*. Why didn't he?

ITEM 11: PIUS XII AND THE REFUGEES

In 1945, Pius approved the use of Vatican money to help German and eastern European refugees, who had fled west to escape the oncoming Soviet army. Many of these refugees had little more than the clothes on their backs. One of the Vatican officials in charge of this program of assistance for refugees was a German bishop named Alois Hudal. Some of the people Hudal helped were Nazis, and some had committed serious crimes. The most famous example was Adolf Eichmann, who was one of the people who supervised the concentration camps. With help from Hudal, he escaped to Argentina. (Years later, he was kidnapped by Israeli commandos, taken to Israel, tried for murder, convicted and hanged.)

Did Pius know that Hudal was helping Nazis? One cannot prove that, but it seems likely.

So why did Pius do it? It is impossible to say for certain, because he never explained it, but it is worth remembering that Herbert Wechsler, a prominent Jewish law professor at Columbia University, was appalled by the thought of punishing people, even though they were Nazis, for doing things that were legal at the time they were done. (Endnote 61) In legal terms, that is referred to as an *ex post facto* law, and the United States Constitution specifically forbids it. That is why, after the American civil war, slaveowners and plantation overseers were not punished for the things they had done when slavery was legal, even though many had committed rape and murder against slaves, and even though punishing them would've been emotionally very satisfying. Abraham Lincoln treated the former slaveowners and plantation overseers the same way Pius treated Eichmann and the others who escaped with Vatican help: let them go, because what they did was legal at the time when they did it.

If you are going to condemn Pius for helping Eichmann, then you must condemn Lincoln too.

Senator Robert Taft of Ohio, a man who came very close to winning the Republican nomination for president in 1952, publicly said in 1946 that there was no way, after a major war, that a trial of the vanquished by the victors can be fair. Taft said the top Nazis should've been treated the same way Napoleon was treated after his defeat: comfortable (but not luxurious) life imprisonment in some remote place. (Endnote 62.)

Pius was an old-fashioned man, like the British government officials who decided exile for life on the island of St. Helena was punishment enough for Napoleon, even though Napoleon had plunged Europe into years of war simply to gratify his own ego. Make no mistake, Napoleon was a villain. There were times when he could've had peace, but he wanted the whole pie and couldn't bear to settle for just a few slices. Hundreds of thousands of people died because of his selfishness. Despite this, he was not given the death penalty. There was an old-fashioned tradition of gentlemanly warfare in Europe whereby, after the fighting was over, the victors and the vanquished would drink a few toasts to each other's bravery, then everybody would go home and nobody would even dream of holding any kind of trial. That's what happened after the American Civil War after all, even though Jefferson Davis, Robert E. Lee, and the rest of the confederates had broken their oath of loyalty to the United States government and were therefore traitors. Pius probably thought sending Eichmann to hide in Argentina for the rest of his life was the equivalent of sending Napoleon to St. Helena, the equivalent of pardoning Davis and Lee.

Pius may also have thought that if war with the USSR broke out, men such as Eichmann could be useful. He was a hard worker, an intelligent man, and a good organizer. If there had been a war between the US and USSR, it is easy to picture Eichmann doing some desk job, efficiently keeping the flow of equipment and supplies going to the troops at the front for Uncle Sam and his allies. He surely would've been willing to help an anti-communist war effort. One could say the same about Mengele. He was a competent medical doctor, after all, and if World War Three had broken out, the allies, naturally, would've needed doctors. America's leaders obviously had similar thoughts. In the years after World War Two, the United States formed an alliance with the Spanish dictator, Francisco Franco, even though Franco had allowed thousands of his soldiers to volunteer to fight alongside Hitler's men against the Soviet Union. President Truman disliked Franco's regime, but America's generals and admirals convinced him that if World War Three broke out, it would be very handy to have American military bases in Spain, so Truman made a deal with Franco. (Endnote 63.)

If you are going to condemn Pius, then you must condemn every American president who was willing to work with Franco: Truman, Eisenhower, Kennedy, Johnson, Nixon, and Ford.

One can see the same pattern in East Asia. Thousands of Japanese committed war crimes, but the American occupation authorities saw fit to give significant punishment to only a few hundred. Forty thousand Chinese prisoners of war were sent to Japan to perform slave labor. Given little food, barefoot and dressed in thin rags even in the bitter cold, they worked in coal mines and did other exhausting jobs. Their lives were about as miserable as human existence can be, and seven thousand died from ill treatment. In one notorious incident, fifty of them were tortured to death by the Japanese after they tried to escape. After Japan surrendered, the murderers of those fifty men were tried and convicted, but none spent more than eight years in prison. The man who was in charge of the slave labor program in that district was punished in no way. Even after Japan surrendered, he continued to be a high-ranking man in the local government. And Kishi Nobusuke, the official in charge of the slave labor program for the entire country, the equivalent of Adolf Eichmann, went on to become prime minister of Japan. (Endnote 64.)

If you are going to condemn Pius for letting Eichmann and Mengele escape, then what can you say about the American authorities who did nothing to punish such horrible crimes in Japan? Harry

Truman knew what was going on. It was no secret. Apparently he had no objection.

And why did the Americans do that? The most likely reason was the desire to keep Japan functioning as an anti-communist bulwark. Pius felt the same way with regard to West Germany. Most Germans, after the war, saw no reason why fellow Germans who had simply obeyed orders during the war should be punished. (Look at the precedent from the American civil war. Henry Wirz, the commandant of the Andersonville POW camp, was convicted of murder after the war and hanged, but none of the guards at Andersonville were put on trial. Everyone took it for granted that only the man at the top was to blame.) The American, British and French insistence on punishing a large number of people had the effect of making America, Britain and France unpopular in West Germany, which could only have had the effect of reducing the enthusiasm of the West German people for an alliance with America, Britain and France. Konrad Adenauer, who served as West Germany's chancellor from 1949 to 1963, worried that West Germany's generals would not cooperate enthusiastically with American, British and French generals as long as there were German military officers in prison. Even the German Social Democratic Party, many of whose members had been murdered by Hitler, thought the three western powers should show more mercy. This is why Pius frequently appealed for clemency for some convicted German war criminals, and why the Americans, British and French eventually halted the prosecutions. (Endnote 65.)

A poll taken in 1950 found that approximately one-third of West Germans thought the Nuremberg trial was unfair. A poll in 1952 found that approximately one-fourth of West Germans had a "good opinion" of Hitler. A poll in 1949 found that a majority of West Germans thought Nazism was "a good idea" that had been "badly applied." (Endnote 66.) In the face of this, what could the American, British and French leaders do? When millions of people insist on thinking a certain way, how can you stop them? When you need their cooperation in the face of the threat from Stalin, you have no choice but to give them some of the things they want, and what they wanted was an end to war crimes prosecutions. Pius XII saw this as clearly as anyone.

Kaiser Wilhelm II started World War One for no good reason, but after the war, he and his top advisors were punished for this in no way. The Germans who had run the war, and who had committed atrocities in Belgium, France and Russia, were anti-communists. The victorious allies were afraid that if they were removed from the scene, no one would be left to lead the German anti-communist movement. Without them, the communists might take over in Germany. So the victorious allies did not prosecute them. As Woodrow Wilson put it at the time, "Had you rather have the kaiser or the Bolsheviks?" (Endnote 67.)

If you are going to condemn Pius, then you must condemn Woodrow Wilson too.

[Editorial note: Wilson said "had" when we today would say "would." That's a good example of how the English language has changed over the years. In the same way, the famous American statesman Henry Clay once said, "I had rather be right than president."]

And of course, you can look at Wernher von Braun, the famous scientist who designed rockets for Hitler that rained death on England. The rockets were built in a factory where the workers were prisoners, worked to the point of exhaustion and death. Von Braun knew that perfectly well, but there is no evidence that he cared. He went to the factory and did his job and averted his eyes from the piles of corpses. The American authorities who let von Braun move to the United States and devote the rest of his life to building rockets for NASA and the

American military did not know about his war-time activities, but that is because they didn't want to know. They asked him no tough questions, and did not investigate him. (Endnote 68.)

It is astonishing to see that even in the 1970s, as von Braun grew ill and approached death, he dashed off a friendly letter to Albert Speer, who had been one of Hitler's top assistants, and who spent twenty years in prison after being convicted in the Nuremberg trial. (Endnote 69.)

And the list goes on. Hubertus Strughold was a NASA scientist who designed the space suit that our astronauts wore on the moon. He also supervised medical experiments in one of Hitler's concentration camps that killed innocent people in various painful ways. United States government officials knew about that when they let him into the country, but he was a genius, and they wanted to have him working for America, so they covered up the truth. (Endnote 70.) Nazi war criminals such as Klaus Barbie, Emil Augsburg, Guido Zimmer and Wilhelm Hoettl also benefited from American government cover-ups. (Endnote 71.)

Our elected officials knew about this. Linda Hunt writes on page 105 of her book, *Secret Agenda: The United States Government, Nazi Scientists, and Project Paperclip, 1945-1980,* that in 1947,

> "... congressmen were listening to testimony that eight hundred Waffen SS officers and other incriminated individuals had entered the United States disguised as political refugees. 'The American authorities have not, in fact, made any attempt even of a superficial nature, to check on the identity of these political refugees,' one critic charged. 'They have, as a matter of record, released collaborationist murderers who have been recognized as such by survivors.' But the congressmen were more worried about Communists than they were about Nazis."

Nothing was done at the time, Hunt writes, to weed out the Nazi war criminals who had snuck into the United States. Not until the 1970s did a significant number of Americans become outraged about this.

Wilhelm Keitel and Alfred Jodl, two of Hitler's top generals, were convicted at the Nuremberg Trial and hanged. Their argument that they only carried out Hitler's orders was rejected. But plenty of other high-ranking German generals, in later trials, were allowed to use that defense. Some of them received only a few years in prison. (Endnote 72.)

How far down does responsibility go? If we are going to prosecute German generals, why not German colonels? Is anyone going to seriously argue that the generals had free will and could be held responsible for the actions, but that the colonels were just robots who had no choice?

Do we imprison the guards at the internment camps for Japanese-Americans in the western United States? Do we say they should've known better? Do we imprison the commandants of those camps? No, we say it was bad but we forgive them and say they were just following orders. John L. DeWitt, the man who was in charge of the Japanese internment program, was never punished. Does anyone seriously think he should have been? He was just following President Roosevelt's orders. Doesn't it make sense to hang just the top people, and give everyone else a pass? You can complain about Pius helping Eichmann escape, but Eichmann was not one of the very high-ranking people in the Nazi regime. His boss, Heinrich Himmler, talked to Hitler frequently, but Eichmann did not.

Obviously, the question of who should be held accountable is not an easy one to answer. Pius favored mercy. Apparently he wanted only the very top people punished. One cannot prove he was wrong to think that way. One has to admit that it is just a matter of opinion.

Then there is the case of Ante Pavelic, the pro-Nazi dictator of Croatia. He lived in Rome for a while after the war, hiding in a Catholic monastery. Surely Pius knew he was there, and surely Pius knew that he had ordered a large number of murders, but all the same, Pius helped him escape to Argentina. Why? We will never know for certain, but it is a fact that the British and Americans also knew Pavelic was hiding in Rome, but did nothing to arrest him and put no serious pressure on Pius to hand him over. Pavelic escaped while the Americans and British deliberately looked the other way. (Endnote 73.) Even Gerald Posner, a man who is by no means friendly to the memory of Pius XII, says on page 140 of his book *God's Bankers* that high-ranking people in the American intelligence community decided to let Pavelic escape. Why did they do that? Once again, it seems unlikely that we will ever know for certain, but one can guess that many anti-communists in Croatia considered Pavelic a hero, and would have lost enthusiasm for the pro-Western cause if the Western powers had hanged their hero. It may be that the Americans, the British and Pius all agreed that because war with Stalin might break out at any minute, it was essential to stay on good terms with all the anti-communist forces in Europe, even the unsavory ones.

They had made an alliance with the murderer Stalin in order to fight Hitler. Now they would make an alliance with Hitler's acolytes to fight Stalin. It was logical, though obviously it did not satisfy the normal human urge for justice.

For any Jews who want to complain about Pius letting war criminals go free, let me point out two names: Yitzhak Shamir and Ariel Sharon.

Shamir was a leading figure in the Stern Gang, a Jewish organization that fought against the British and the Arabs in Palestine in the 1940s when the British were the colonial power. The United Nations sent a Swedish diplomat, Count Folke Bernadotte, to try to mediate a cease-fire between the Jews and the Arabs. The Stern Gang believed that a cease-fire at that point was not in the best interests of the Jewish people, so the leaders, including Shamir, unanimously voted to kill Bernadotte. And so it was done. Bernadotte was assassinated by the Stern Gang in 1948. Shamir was punished for this cold-blooded murder in no way. He went on to become prime minister of Israel. One can read about this in Shamir's obituary in the July 1, 2012 issue of the *Washington Post*, and also in the Wikipedia articles about Bernadotte and Shamir. Yehoshua Cohen, the man who pulled the trigger and killed Bernadotte, was never punished.

Boy, it takes a lot of gall for anyone to castigate Pius XII, while saying nothing about Shamir and the other hoodlums who got off scot-free after they murdered Bernadotte, a man who only wanted peace. But that is what Goldhagen does.

And Ariel Sharon? The Israeli commission that investigated the massacre of Palestinians in the Sabra and Shatila refugee camps in 1982 found that Sharon, who was defense minister at the time, was "indirectly responsible," and should be fired. (Endnote 74.) Israel had invaded Lebanon and was occupying the part of Lebanon in which Sabra and Shatila were located. The massacre was carried out by the Phalangists, an armed faction in Lebanon that was allied with Israel. The commission determined that Sharon allowed the Phalangists to enter Sabra and Shatila to look for Palestinian terrorists and weapons, even though it was common knowledge that the Phalangists often massacred their enemies and hated the Palestinians. Naturally, a massacre ensued.

The commission found no evidence that Sharon actually wanted a massacre. Of course, what evidence could prove such a thing? One cannot read Sharon's mind, and he would never be stupid enough to openly tell people (except perhaps a few like-minded friends who would never testify against him) that he wanted hundreds of defenseless Palestinian civilians butchered. But the commission pointed out that Jews have always blamed pogroms not just on the perpetrators, but also on government officials who could have stopped the pogroms but did not. In this sense, the commission declared, Sharon and some of his subordinates were guilty. (Endnote 75.)

Amos Oz, a famous Israeli novelist, put it well: "One who invites the Boston strangler to spend two nights in an orphanage cannot claim, when he sees a pile of dead bodies the next morning, that he had asked the man only to wash the ears and necks of the orphans." (Endnote 76.)

We all know that in war, civilians get caught in the crossfire sometimes, but this was no accident, and there was no justification for it. Thomas Friedman, a Jewish-American journalist who covered the Middle East for years for the *New York Times*, saw the victims with his own eyes. They were women, old men, young men with their hands tied behind their backs. He estimates the number killed at between eight hundred and a thousand. He saw no excuse for Sharon's behavior. (Endnote 77.) Neither did the editors of the *New Republic*, an ardently Zionist magazine. (Endnote 78.)

But despite this, Sharon did not spend a single day in jail, and went on to become Israel's prime minister. Does Goldhagen think it was awful that Eichmann was allowed to escape, but okay that Sharon got off scot-free? In his book, *A Moral Reckoning*, he refuses to even discuss the issue.

Ah, but then, years later, he finally did discuss the issue. On pages 341-342 of his book *The Devil that Never Dies*, Goldhagen rants about how awful he thinks it is that some British newspaper printed a cartoon that depicted Ariel Sharon as a brutal murderer. He doesn't say a word about Sharon's victims. He doesn't even admit that Sharon had any victims. He doesn't try to prove Sharon was innocent, because, of course, he can't. For no particular reason, he just tells us that we should feel sorry for the murderer. Goldhagen ignores hundreds of murder victims and oozes sympathy for the murderer.

I'm sure there are some people in the United States who are on a lower moral level than Goldhagen, but fortunately, there aren't many.

ITEM 12: WHAT CAUSES ANTISEMITISM?

Goldhagen, in *A Moral Reckoning,* says Pius XII and many other Catholic prelates were to blame for stirring up the antisemitism that led to the Holocaust. David Kertzer makes the same argument in his book *The Popes Against the Jews: The Vatican's Role in the Rise of Modern Anti-Semitism*, though he mostly blames Catholic intellectual journals, especially an Italian one called *La Civilta Cattolica.*

There certainly were Catholics in those days who stirred up hostility towards Jews. Pius XII was not among them, but he could've cracked down on them, and he never did. That was a shortcoming in his leadership, but of course, every leader has shortcomings. Do we denounce Thomas Jefferson today because he never said we should give women the right to vote? Do we denounce Franklin Roosevelt because he never insisted that automobiles have seat belts and never proposed any plan to give voting rights to southern blacks? Nobody foresaw that something like the Holocaust was going to happen someday, and the fact that there was job discrimination against Jews in Europe just didn't seem like all that big a deal. There was lots of job discrimination against Catholics in the United States and Great Britain in those days too, and I never heard of Pius complaining about that either. I remember Mario Cuomo said that after he graduated from law school, he couldn't get a job with a prestigious New York City law firm, because such firms simply would not hire an Italian. I never heard of any pope complaining about that.

If you want to hear about discrimination, just look at the fact that wealthy Jews, when they were hiring servants, used to discriminate against their fellow Jews. They wanted gentile servants, because gentiles were willing to work on the Jewish sabbath. You can read about this on the website of "The YIVO Encyclopedia of Jews in Eastern Europe" in an article titled "Servants," written by a scholar named Judith Kalik. What rabbi ever denounced wealthy Jews for doing that? What rabbi ever declared "It is a sin to discriminate against your own people!" None that I ever heard of. Kalik's article doesn't mention any rabbi opposing this practice, though it does mention that, for a while, the Catholic Church opposed it. (But poor Catholics needed jobs, so eventually the Church relented and allowed them to work for Jews.)

There is a British comedian named Tracey Ullman. She used to have an HBO sketch comedy series called *Tracey Takes On*, and she wrote a book with the same title, full of transcripts from that HBO series. The book contains several jokes about how greedy and money-obsessed East Asians supposedly are. I guess if Ullman had been living a hundred and fifty years ago, she would've been telling jokes about how greedy and money-obsessed Jews supposedly are. Are we going to condemn Tracey Ullman? Are we going to say she should stop telling jokes about East Asians today because that might lead to a holocaust?

Furthermore, we have to ask ourselves, even if some Catholic bishops and priests were antisemitic, how important were they in stirring up antisemitism compared to other factors? Some people seem to think Christianity is the one and only cause of antisemitism, but that is far from true. It seems to me that there are several causes. One is simple envy. Jews are conspicuously successful in many walks of life, and people who aren't terribly successful resent them for it. They think, "I break my back doing manual labor, and the Jews make big money as doctors and lawyers and accountants and they never do any hard work. Is that fair? Isn't this my country?"

Second, look at the fact that George Orwell interviewed some antisemites in England during the World War Two for an essay that he wrote, and he said none of them cited religious reasons for their views. Instead they claimed Jews were dodging the draft and violating the rationing laws. Orwell also thought it was significant that Jews were often small shopkeepers and therefore seemed like exploiters to blue-collar gentiles. (Endnote 79.)

Steven Pinker, the prominent Harvard psychology professor, made the same point on page 235 of his book *The Blank Slate*. He pointed out that throughout history, all over the world, people have resented the store owner, the middle man, because he gets a profit yet does not seem to produce anything nor do any hard work. This, Pinker says, has resulted in persecution of Jews, of Chinese (in Vietnam, Malaysia, and Indonesia), of Lebanese (in Africa), of Armenians (in the Turkish empire) and of the "Gujeratis and Chettyars of India."

Third, if antisemitism is caused by Christianity, why are there atheist antisemites? The king of the atheists in the nineteenth century was Karl Marx, and he once wrote, "What is the worldly cult of the Jew? Huckstering. What is his worldly god? Money." (Endnote 80.) Another prominent nineteenth century atheist, Pierre-Joseph Proudhon, one of the founding fathers of anarchism, was even more blunt. "The Jew is the enemy of the human race," Proudhon wrote. "One must send this race back to Asia or exterminate it." (Endnote 81.) Marx and Proudhon were not alone. Quite a few of the nineteenth century's most outspoken antisemites were atheists, agnostics and secularists. (Endnote 82.) H.G. Wells, the famous science fiction writer, was an atheist, as any biography of the man will tell you. Wells also wanted to exterminate the Jews, the blacks, and the Asians. (Endnote 83.) Voltaire, the leading figure of the Enlightenment, was antisemitic. Speaking of the Jews, he once wrote, "I would not be in the least bit surprised if these people would not someday become deadly to the human race." (Endnote 84.) Near the end of Voltaire's novella *Candide*, Candide is swindled out of all his money by "the Jews." Voltaire seems to have considered that to be what one would naturally expect from Jews. Also, all historians agree that the leading antisemite in France in the years between the world wars was an atheist named Charles Maurras, the leader of the Action Francaise organization and editor-in-chief of a daily newspaper called *L'Action Francaise*. He described the Christian gospels as phony stories written by "four shabby Jews" and Christianity as a religion for the "rabble." (Endnote 85.)

Here in the United States, the most influential atheist or agnostic of the twentieth century was surely H.L. Mencken, and he once said, when discussing World War One, that Jews had "robbed the plain people on a colossal scale during the war." (Endnote 86.) Then, in November 1938, when letting Jewish refugees into the United States became a controversial issue, Mencken said he favored letting German Jews in, because they were a "superior group," but did not favor letting in eastern European Jews. (Endnote 87.)

And here's another statement by Mencken about Jews:

"As commonly encountered, they strike other people as predominantly unpleasant, and everywhere on Earth they seem to be disliked. This dislike, despite their own belief to the contrary, has nothing to do with their religion: it is founded, rather, on their bad manners, their curious lack of tact. They have an extraordinary capacity for offending and alarming the Goyim." (Endnote 88.)

("Goyim" is a Jewish word that means "gentiles.")

George Orwell saw this too, though he, too, wasn't the least bit religious. In his essay "Anti-Semitism in Britain," he quotes a "middle-class woman" as saying, "the way these Jews behave is too absolutely stinking. The way they push their way to the head of queues, and so on. They're so abominably selfish. I think they're responsible for a lot of what happens to them." (Endnote 89.)

In the diary he kept during World War Two, Orwell made similar observations. In one spot he wrote, "What is bad about Jews is that they are not only conspicuous, but go out of their way to make themselves so. A fearful Jewish woman, a regular comic-paper cartoon of a Jewess, fought her way off the train at Oxford Circus, landing blows on anyone who stood in her way. It took me back to old days on the Paris Metro." (Endnote 90.) Elsewhere he wrote that the "tactlessness" of some Jewish refugees in Britain was "almost incredible." (Endnote 91.)

Deborah Tannen, a famous professor of linguistics, made a similar point in her bestselling book, *You Just Don't Understand: Women and Men in Conversation*. She said Jews consider it normal to interrupt people in conversation, but gentiles think interrupting is rude, and therefore think Jews are rude.

And of course, there is the simple fact that none of the top Nazis was a churchgoer. None of the books by militant atheists names a single one who was, and surely they would if they could. John Cornwell devoted his book *Hitler's Pope* to slinging mud at Pope Pius XII, very unfairly in my opinion, but even Cornwell admits, on page 116 of the hardcover edition, that in 1930, the Vatican's official newspaper printed an editorial that said Catholics were not allowed to belong to the Nazi Party.

So, just to repeat what I said earlier, how can antisemitism be blamed on the Christian churches when so many atheists and agnostics are antisemitic?

Fourth, look at the book, *Antisemitism*, by the famous Jewish philosopher Hannah Arendt, published by Harcourt, Brace and World, Incorporated, in 1968. On pages 35-36, we read, "The simultaneous rise of antisemitism as a serious political factor in Germany, Austria and France in the last twenty years of the nineteenth century was preceded by a series of financial scandals and fraudulent affairs" in which Jews were involved. Jews were only "middlemen," Arendt writes, but she notes that in France, the "lower middle classes" suffered the most from these scandals. Many Frenchmen lost their life savings, and they "turned antisemitic."

On pages 95-96 of *Antisemitism*, Arendt goes into more detail. A French company was trying to build a canal in Panama, and to raise money, it sold bonds to the general public to the tune of 1.335 billion francs. The press, the majority in Parliament and many high-ranking government officials were all bribed to publicly say everything was fine and the bonds were a good investment. In 1892, when the truth about the complete failure of the canal-building plan came to light, approximately half a million middle-class Frenchmen were financially wiped out. Two Jews, Jacques Reinach and Cornelius Herz, had been payed to hand out the bribes to the Parliamentarians. "Naturally there were quite a number of smaller Jewish businessmen working for both Herz and Reinach," Arendt notes.

The news spread. Soon all of Europe was talking about how Jews had perpetrated a gigantic swindle in France. No one can doubt that the Panama scandal did a lot to build the walls of Auschwitz, but guys like Goldhagen and Kertzer ignore it as if it was a trivial incident. Instead they rant on and on about antisemitic statements in Catholic intellectual journals.

In Austria, a major outcry erupted in the 1880s because of a peculiar situation in the railroad industry. Look at page 43 of Hannah Arendt's book *Antisemitism* and you will see that the "major part" of Austria's railroads had been in the hands of the Jewish Rothschild family since 1836. (The Rothschilds were bankers, and the Habsburgs gave them a "license" to run the railroads in exchange for loans.) An antisemitic rabble-rouser wanted the railroads nationalized in 1886 when the license expired, but instead the government tried to extend the license on terms that were, in Arendt's words, "patently to the disadvantage of the state as well as the public." People all over the Austrian empire started grumbling that the government was controlled by the Jews. Into this atmosphere, Hitler was born.

So this is the way Kertzer and Goldhagen think: Catholic newspapers can influence people, but massive scandals can't.

Fifth, as I said earlier, Saul Friedlander is a history professor at UCLA and won a Pulitzer Prize years ago with a massive book about the Holocaust called *The Years of Extermination: Nazi Germany and the Jews, 1939-1945*. On page 109 of that book, Friedlander writes that one of the reasons why antisemitism became more common in France in the 1930s was because of "a series of financial-political scandals in which some Jews were conspicuously implicated."

(The other reasons for antisemitism in France, according to Friedlander, were tradition, Nazi propaganda, the fact that conservatives disliked a Jewish socialist named Leon Blum who briefly served as prime minister, and "massive immigration of foreign Jews." According to Friedlander, even French Jews had negative feelings about the German Jews and eastern European Jews who were immigrating to France.)

Sixth, there was a French Jew named Irene Nemirovsky who spent the 1920s and 1930s writing bestselling novels that depicted Jews as being greedy beyond belief. (Endnote 92.) And if you want to talk about novels, look at *Oliver Twist* by Charles Dickens. Without a doubt, *Oliver Twist* makes Jews look bad. (One must keep in mind that in the movie, *Oliver!*, Fagin really isn't such a bad guy, but in the novel, he is a cold-blooded murderer.) Fagin is a horrible villain, and Dickens frequently refers to him simply as "the Jew." If the entertainment industry has any ability at all to influence human attitudes, then surely a popular novel by England's most popular novelist of the nineteenth century must have had some impact. Surely *Oliver Twist* was translated into foreign languages. It was so popular in Britain, why would it not be? Then in 1922, a silent movie version was made, with Lon Chaney as Fagin and Jackie Coogan as Oliver. According to Wikipedia, it got an enthusiastic review in the *New York Times*, and I bet it was translated into German, Italian, French and who knows what else. Why would it not be, when it was so easy to translate silent films into foreign languages? David Kertzer talks on and on about antisemitic statements that he found in Catholic intellectual journals in the late 1800s and early 1900s, but I bet the 1922 *Oliver Twist* movie was more influential than all of those journals combined.

So this is how Kertzer and Goldhagen think: Catholic newspapers can influence people, but bestselling novels and popular movies can't.

And surely we have all heard of *The Merchant of Venice*, Hitler's favorite Shakespeare play.

Seventh, look at the fact that Henry Ford, the famous automaker, one of the richest and most admired men in the world in the first half of the twentieth century, was a hard-core antisemite, certain that Jews were conspiring to take over the world. His book, *The International Jew*, was translated into sixteen languages, and, according to Wikipedia, six editions of it were published in Germany from 1920 to 1922. Hitler, in his book *Mein Kampf,* sang Ford's praises. According to the book *Henry Ford and the Jews: The Mass Production of Hate* by Neil Baldwin, Ford grew up in a conventional Protestant family, but he doesn't seem to have been particularly religious in adulthood. One wonders why Goldhagen and the other people who constantly bash Pius XII ignore him. Do they find it impossible to imagine that Ford might've been influential?

Here, I must explain that antisemites in Russia in the early twentieth century concocted a document called *The Protocols of the Elders of Zion*, which was purported to describe the secret plan of a group of Jewish conspirators to take over the world. This hoax received little attention until Ford got hold of it. He believed *The Protocols* were genuine, and discussed them extensively in *The International Jew.* A historian named Norman Cohn has declared, "All in all, *The International Jew* probably did more than any other work to make the *Protocols* famous." (Endnote 93.) Baldur von Schirach, who eventually was appointed by Hitler to lead the Hitler Youth, once said, "The younger generation looked with envy to the symbols of success and prosperity like Henry Ford. And if Henry Ford said that the Jews were to blame, why, naturally we believed him." (Endnote 94.)

In 1938, Hitler awarded Ford the highest award the Nazis gave to foreigners, the Grand Service Cross of the Supreme Order of the German Eagle. The German consul in Cleveland gave it to Ford at Ford's birthday dinner in Detroit before an audience of 1,500 people. (Endnote 95.)

Eighth, conservatives are sometimes antisemitic because they think Jews are a bunch of communists. It is certainly true that in Europe and in the United States, Jews were more likely than gentiles to join communist groups or other extreme left-wing groups. Robert Wistrich, a history professor whom I mentioned earlier, has written that the "high visibility" of Jews in the German left-wing revolutionary movement right after World War One "was a key element in the revival of antisemitism on the Right." (Endnote 96.) Orwell noticed that even orthodox communists were sometimes antisemitic because they disliked Trotskyists and anarchists, and "Trotskyists and anarchists tend to be Jews." (Endnote 97.) Just look at the fact that the Soviet politburo (ruling committee) in 1922 had seven members, and three of them were Jews: Trotsky, Kamenev, and Zinoviev. (Endnote 98.) It is amazing that such a thing could happen when only a small percentage of the people in the Soviet empire were Jewish.

The renowned historian Saul Friedlander has unearthed a statistic that is even more startling. The Soviet government kept track of people by ethnic group, and in 1934, the highest-ranking people in the Soviet secret police were thirty-seven Jews, thirty Russians, seven Latvians, five Ukrainians, four Poles, three Georgians, three Belorussians, two Germans, and five others. (Endnote 99.)

It is also a fact that in the 1931 census in Poland, 9.7 percent of the population was Jewish. Yet, in 1932, the Polish communist party, which had a separate bureau for members who spoke Yiddish only, recorded that 24 percent of its members spoke only Yiddish. (Endnote 100.)

Ninth, many leftists disliked Jews because, in their opinion, Jews were a bunch of greedy capitalists. Robert Wistrich reports on pages 118 to 121 of his book, *A Lethal Obsession: Anti-Semitism from Antiquity to the Global Jihad*, that in the late 1800s and early 1900s, *Justice*, the official newspaper of the British Social Democratic Federation, often editorialized about the evil "capitalist Jew," and blamed the Boer War on the machinations of a small "Jew clique" of bankers who had dragged Britain into the "Jew war in the Transvaal" in order get their hands on gold and diamond mines. In September 1900, the Trades Union Congress in the Great Britain adopted a resolution that said the Boer War was designed "to secure the gold fields of South Africa for cosmopolitan Jews," most of whom had "no patriotism and no country."

Do Kertzer and Goldhagen seriously think British socialists thought that way because they were influenced by the Catholic Church? I think it is safe to say that British socialists in those days didn't care a flying fig about what the Catholic Church thought about anything.

(Did Jewish businessmen bribe British politicians to start the Boer War, just so they could make a big profit? I have no idea.)

Then there is Rosa Luxemburg, a prominent Jewish communist philosopher who was killed shortly after World War One during a communist uprising in Germany. She blamed antisemitism on the dishonesty of Jewish businessmen, saying, "what is usually described and persecuted as 'Judaism' is nothing but the spirit of hucksterism and swindle, which appears in every society where exploitation reigns." She believed that once capitalism was abolished, antisemitism would fade away. (Endnote 101.)

In a similar vein, Supreme Court Justice Louis Brandeis, who was Jewish, once said in a letter to a friend that he and some of his friends had stopped making donations to the World Zionist Organization because it was dominated by Russian Jews who "like many Russian Jews in this country – don't know what honesty is & we simply won't entrust our money to them." (Endnote 102.)

That is really startling. A man like Brandeis would surely not make an accusation like that if he didn't think it was supported by solid evidence.

Or are Kertzer and Goldhagen going to argue that Brandeis was brainwashed by reading Catholic intellectual journals?

Tenth, look at the book, *Tough Jews: Fathers, Sons, and Gangster Dreams*, by Rich Cohen. It's a look at prominent Jewish gangsters, such as Arnold Rothstein, Bugsy Siegel, Meyer Lansky, Dutch Schultz (whose real name was Arthur Flegenheimer), and Bo Weinberg.

Every honest person must admit that the story of organized crime in the United States, east of the Mississippi River, is mostly a story of Italians and Jews. Italian participation in organized crime led to anti-Italian sentiment. Just look at the way eleven Italian immigrants were lynched in New Orleans in 1891 for allegedly assassinating the chief of police. (Endnote 103.) Therefore it is not the least bit surprising that Jewish participation in organized crime led to antisemitism. Other than the Italians, who but the Jews produced so many Mafia bigshots? Look at the famous movies made about Jewish gangsters, such as *Bugsy*, *Billy Bathgate*, and *Once Upon a Time in America*. Did anyone ever make a movie about a German immigrant or a Norwegian immigrant or a Polish immigrant who became a gangster? I've never heard of one.

Eleventh, if one agrees with Goldhagen and Kertzer that the Catholic Church is to blame for stirring up antisemitism, then why was there so much antisemitism in the Protestant countries? Look at pages 302 and 303 of the book, *The Last Million: Europe's Displaced Persons from World War to Cold War*, by David Nasaw. Nasaw tells us that as of January 1, 1947, there were between 200,000 and 250,000 Jewish refugees still living in refugee camps in Germany, and the allies had no idea of where to put them. Many of them had been born in eastern

Europe, but they did not want to return there, out of fear of Stalin, or out of fear of antisemitism. But Nasaw makes it clear that no country in the West wanted them. Not the Netherlands, not the United States, not Canada, not Australia, not Great Britain, not France, not Sweden, not Norway, not Denmark, not Finland. Nobody volunteered to take in the Jews, not even a few thousand of them. Personally, Truman would've been willing to let them immigrate to the United States, but Congress opposed it, so there was nothing he could do.

One often hears American liberals sing the praises of Scandinavia. If Scandinavia is so wonderful, why were the Scandinavian countries unwilling to take in the Jewish refugees?

The Jewish refugees themselves were willing to go to Palestine, and the Jews in Palestine were willing to take them in, but the Arabs in Palestine most certainly were not, so the British, in the years immediately after World War Two, allowed very few Jews to move to Palestine, for fear of upsetting the Arabs. But eventually the British got tired of refereeing the conflict between the Arabs and the Jews in Palestine. They threw up their hands, pulled out their troops and let the Arabs and Jews fight it out. The Jews won the war, and the new Israeli government took in the Jewish refugees. Truman himself told his advisors that he was going to recognize the new state of Israel because, among other reasons, it was the only feasible place to put the Jewish refugees. (Endnote 104.)

Twelfth, Albert Einstein was born in Ulm, Germany, in 1879. There were no public schools in Ulm in those days, so his parents sent him to a Catholic school. Years later, in adulthood, he declared that he encountered no significant antisemitism there. Nor did he encounter any in Switzerland, Italy or Prague when he lived in those places. Not until he moved to Berlin, a mostly Protestant city, did he encounter any significant antisemitism. (Endnote 105.)

If the Catholic Church in those days was a machine dedicated to flooding the world with antisemitism, as Kertzer and Goldhagen allege, why did Einstein fail to notice?

ITEM 13: GOLDHAGEN GETS THE FACTS WRONG

On page 49 of *A Moral Reckoning*, Goldhagen talks about a Vatican radio broadcast that occurred in January 1940. Goldhagen says that broadcast talked about the sufferings of Poles in Poland, but said nothing about the suffering of Jews in Poland. This, Goldhagen says, is a smoking gun. This, he says, proves that Pius XII cared about gentile suffering but did not care about Jewish suffering.

But once again, Goldhagen is wrong. He says he read about this broadcast on page 75 of a book called *Pius XII and the Second World War* by a historian named Pierre Blet, so I looked at that page in that book, and it doesn't say what Goldhagen claims it says. Blet mentions that broadcast, and he quotes a few sentences from it, but he never says that broadcast failed to mention Jewish suffering. Michael Phayer, on the other hand, a historian whom Goldhagen quotes elsewhere, has said that that broadcast definitely did mention the sufferings of the Jews of Poland. It said both Jews and Poles in Poland were being terrorized by the Germans and faced "starvation" because the Germans had confiscated so much of Poland's food supply. (Endnote 106.)

Isn't it amazing that Goldhagen so badly misunderstood what Blet wrote? One has to wonder if he deliberately was trying to deceive his readers.

ITEM 14: THE BELIEFS OF DAVID BEN-GURION

David Ben-Gurion was the leader of the Zionist movement in Palestine during World War Two. Later, he became the first prime minister of Israel. During World War Two, he said something astonishing. He said, "If I knew that it was possible to save all the children in Germany by transporting them to England, but only half of them by transporting them to Palestine, I would chose the second – because we face not only the reckoning of those children, but the historical reckoning of the Jewish people." You can find that quote on page 28 of the book *The Seventh Million: The Israelis and the Holocaust*, by Tom Segev.

(By "children in Germany," he meant the Jewish children in Germany.)

Ben-Gurion, obviously, thought building up a Jewish state in Palestine was more important than rescuing Jewish children. Can you imagine how militant atheists would be screaming their heads off today if Pius XII had ever said anything like that?

Let me ask Goldhagen and all of Pius's other critics this question: if saving Jewish lives wasn't the number one priority for David Ben-Gurion, why should it have been the number one priority for Pius XII? And if Goldhagen is going to angrily denounce Pius XII, why does he not denounce Ben-Gurion?

And look at this: a Jewish group in the United States started a petition drive to ask the British to set up refugee camps for tens of thousands of Hungarian Jews in Palestine (which was a British colony in those days) with the promise that they would be forced to leave Palestine after the war. (As I said earlier, the reason why the British didn't want to let lots of Jewish refugees go to Palestine was because they feared the Arabs would revolt when they saw more Jews entering the country. The promise that the Jews would leave after the war was meant to reassure the Arabs.) Five hundred thousand Americans signed that petition, and it was presented to Congress by a group of rabbis and a Greek Orthodox archbishop. But astonishingly, most American Zionist leaders opposed that petition. They could not bear to promise that some Jews would not have the right to live permanently in Palestine. You can read about this on page 253 of the critically-acclaimed book, *The Abandonment of the Jews: America and the Holocaust, 1941-1945*, by David S. Wyman.

If saving Jewish lives wasn't the number one priority for most American Zionist leaders, why should it have been the number one priority for Pius XII? And why does Goldhagen not mention this? Wyman published *The Abandonment of the Jews* long before Goldhagen published his book about Pius XII, so you can't say Goldhagen had no opportunity to read about it.

The simple fact is that getting Jews out of Hitler's empire was not much of a problem. There were ways to do that. The problem was where to put them. Believe it or not, Anthony Eden, the British foreign minister for most of the war, actually said that he was afraid Hitler might offer to let the Allies take the Jews. There was no way the British government wanted more Jewish refugees in Great Britain, and it could think of no other good place to put them either, so this would be embarrassing for the British government. You can read about this on pages 97 thru 99 of *The Abandonment of the Jews* by David S. Wyman.

Alas, the American government showed no courage on this matter either. With a snap of his fingers, Franklin Roosevelt could have saved the lives of 180,000 more Jews by granting them refugee status and letting them into the United States. The law allowed that. But he didn't do it. He feared it would be politically unpopular. You can read about this on page 136 of *The Abandonment of the Jews* by David S. Wyman.

Why is it then, that you don't see half as much invective hurled at Franklin Roosevelt as you see hurled at Pius XII?

ITEM 15: COLLABORATORS

A Jew named Primo Levi survived Auschwitz and wrote a book about his experiences that was published in the United States under the title *Survival in Auschwitz*. (In other countries, it was called *If This Is a Man*.) It became an international bestseller and was translated into several languages. In this book, he openly admits that he survived Auschwitz because he collaborated with the Germans. Some German scientists were doing research at Auschwitz, trying to find a way to manufacture synthetic rubber. They needed an assistant, and because Levi had a doctoral degree in chemistry, he got the job. This allowed him to get extra food and to avoid doing heavy manual labor outdoors in the bitter cold. It saved his life, and the fact that he was helping the German war effort apparently did not bother him. He was working to kill the Allied soldiers who were trying to rescue him.

I've never heard Goldhagen nor anyone else criticize Levi for doing this.

Let us be blunt. Levi helped the Nazis. Nobody says Pius helped the Nazis. They only complain that he didn't do enough to hurt them. So why does Pius get so much criticism while Levi gets none?

And of course, Levi wasn't alone. Read *Remembering Survival: Inside a Nazi Slave Labor Camp*, by the famous historian Christopher Browning, a book which won the National Jewish Book Award. Browning tells us that thousands of Jews worked in Hitler's weapons factories, doing their best to kill Soviet, American and British soldiers. But Kertzer and Goldhagen never admit that. I would like to ask them, if it was okay for thousands of Jews to collaborate with Hitler because they thought that would improve their chances of survival, why was it not okay for Pius XII to keep silent so that Hitler would not kill a hundred thousand Polish gentiles in reprisal?

ITEM 16: GERALD POSNER

A few years ago, Gerald Posner, a prominent author of nonfiction books, wrote a book called *God's Bankers: A History of Money and Power at the Vatican*. It accuses Pius XII and other popes of various sleazy activities having to do with Vatican financial matters. However, I don't think the book can be taken seriously, because there are obvious mistakes in it, and naturally this makes one wonder if Posner can be trusted to keep the facts straight when he reports on the complicated financial matters that are at the heart of the book.

First, the most obvious mistake is on page 99, where Posner tells us that the king of Italy in 1943 was a man named Emmanuel III. The truth is that the man's name in English was Victor Emmanuel III, which in Italian is Vittorio Emanuele III. Any biography of Mussolini will mention his correct name, and so does Wikipedia, and so does *The Rise and Fall of the Third Reich*, by William L. Shirer, a book that sold millions of copies worldwide.

When I was in journalism school, we got an automatic F on any assignment in which we reported someone's name incorrectly. Let me say once again, if Posner can't get such a simple fact right, how can we trust him to report accurately about the complicated financial matters that are at the heart of *God's Bankers*? Would you trust a book about American history that said the president of the United States from 1969 to 1974 was a man named Milhous Nixon?

Second, look at pages 141 and 142. Posner says there that Romania, Bulgaria, Macedonia, Montenegro, Serbia and Bosnia-Hercegovina are Catholic countries. That isn't true, and any encyclopedia will tell you so. Bosnia-Hercegovina has a sizable Catholic minority, about 15 percent of the population, but the other five countries don't even have that much. It is absolutely astonishing that a prominent writer such as Posner, a man who has been on the bestsellers list, would make such an error, in a book whose main subject is the Catholic church. A college professor would laugh at any student who made that mistake in a term paper.

Third, also on pages 141 and 142, Posner says that after World War Two, "Six Catholic-dominated nations that had won a temporary independence between the world wars – Croatia, Macedonia, Montenegro, Serbia, Slovenia, and Bosnia and Herzegovina – were united under the banner of Yugoslavia and the iron-fisted rule of its communist leader, Tito." Posner is saying here that Yugoslavia didn't exist between the world wars. That is false. After World War One, the British, French and Americans rewarded their Serbian ally by letting the Serbs annex Slovenia, Croatia, Montenegro and Bosnia-Hercegovina, thus forming Yugoslavia. This too is information that can be found in any good encyclopedia. Just look up "Yugoslavia."

Fourth, on page 11, Posner writes that Pope Pius VI approved a certain man to be "Italy's Prime Minister," but then this prime minister "imposed a tax on church properties."

That can't possibly be true. Throughout the 1700s, there was no country called "Italy." In those days, Italy was divided up into several small independent countries. Any professor of Italian history, or of Napoleonic history, can tell you that it was not until the early 1800s that Napoleon consolidated some of those small countries into one country, named it "the Republic of Italy," and made it a satellite of France. But Pope Pius VI could not possibly have approved the appointment of someone to be prime minister of the Republic of Italy, because Pius VI died in 1799, years before Napoleon did that. (Endnote 107.)

Fifth, on page 71, Posner writes that Pius XII, in 1936, when he was still just the Vatican's secretary of state, visited the United States. That much is true. Posner says Pius met with President Roosevelt one day after FDR was re-elected. That is also true. Posner says FDR was "concerned" about a Catholic priest named Charles Coughlin. That may be true. Coughlin had a weekly radio show in which he talked about politics, and he frequently criticized FDR. Then Posner says the "results" of the meeting were this: "Two days after the meeting, Coughlin announced the last broadcast of his provocative show that reached thirty million listeners."

Clearly, Posner is trying to create the impression that FDR pressured the Vatican to muzzle Coughlin, and that the Vatican complied. That is not true. The truth is that in 1936, Coughlin supported a left-wing third party candidate named William Lemke for president, and Coughlin promised repeatedly that he would give up broadcasting if Lemke received fewer than 9 million votes. Lemke did not even come close to getting 9 million votes, so Coughlin kept his promise and gave up broadcasting. Pressure from the Vatican or from FDR had nothing to do with it. Furthermore, several weeks later, in 1937, Coughlin started broadcasting again. He quit again in late 1937. He resumed again in 1938. He went off the air for good in 1940, because radio stations started refusing to sell him air time, because of complaints that he was antisemitic. (Endnote 108.)

Sixth, Posner says on page 71 that Charles Coughlin was "bigoted" in 1936. Not so. He didn't start making antisemitic statements until 1938. (Endnote 109.)

Seventh, Posner says on page 10 that there is something in Rome called "St. Peter's cathedral." Wrong. That big church is called St. Peter's basilica. A Catholic church building is a cathedral only if a pope officially gives it that status, and no pope has ever done that for St. Peter's basilica.

Eighth, on page 109, Posner writes, "Many devout Catholics maintained their faith at the same time they worked at concentration camps and ran the Third Reich's bureaucracy of mass murder." That is a barefaced lie. Posner has no source of information to back up that claim, because there is none. In the years since 1945, many Germans have been convicted of taking part in the Holocaust, but I have never heard of a single one who was a "devout Catholic." I have read the books of the militant atheists, such as Richard Dawkins, Christopher Hitchens, Sam Harris, Carl Sagan and A.C. Grayling, and even they never name any German Catholics who took part in the Holocaust. Surely they would if they could. Look at the book *Hitler's People: The Faces of the Third Reich*, by Richard J. Evans, a prominent British history professor. In the whole book, Evans does not name any German Catholics who took part in the Holocaust. On pages 186, 264 and 268 of his critically-acclaimed book *Bloodlands: Europe Between Hitler and Stalin*, the famous Yale historian Timothy Snyder writes that the Germans recruited over a million Soviet POWs to serve as guards in the death camps and help kill Jews in other ways. The people shooting the Jews, rounding up the Jews, pushing them into the gas chambers, and guarding the camps were, overwhelmingly, Soviet POWs, not Germans. The Soviet Union was certainly not a Catholic country, so few if any of those Soviet POWs could have been Catholics.

It is amazing that Posner had the gall to tell such a barefaced lie.

Ninth, in 1933, the Vatican and Hitler's government signed a treaty known in Germany as the Reichskonkordat, which specified what the legal rights and obligations of the Catholic Church were going to be in Germany. On page 65, Posner says that it gave the Catholic church an annual subsidy from the German government, which is true. Many governments in Europe in those days subsidized this or that religious group, and some still do. Then, also on page 65, Posner writes, "In return, the Vatican gave Hitler the formal endorsement he wanted." That is ridiculous. Look at the book *Hitler's Pope*, by John Cornwell. Cornwell spends the whole book slinging mud at Pius XII, quite unfairly in my opinion, but even he admits on page 153 that shortly after the Reichskonkordat was signed, Pius XII, who was Cardinal Pacelli at the time, wrote an article for the Vatican's official newspaper that said signing the Reichskonkordat definitely did not mean the Vatican or the church or the pope approved of Hitler's policies.

Tenth, on page 65, Posner tells us that "Article 16 of the Reichskonkordat required German bishops and cardinals to swear an oath of loyalty to the Third Reich." That is not true, if "loyalty" means total, unquestioning obedience. Look at the book *The Catholic Church and Nazi Germany*, by the famous Jewish historian Guenter Lewy. On page 82, Lewy writes that Article 16 of the Reichskonkordat said new bishops "had to swear to respect the government and cause their clergy to do the same. 'In the due solicitude for the welfare and the interests of the German Reich,' they were, while performing their spiritual office, 'to prevent anything which might threaten to be detrimental to it.'" But that leaves open the question of what the "welfare and the interests of the German Reich" were. On pages 291 and 292, Lewy states that in August 1943, a joint pastoral letter of the German Catholic bishops "reminded the faithful that the killing of innocents was wrong even if done by the authorities and allegedly for the common good, as in the case of 'men of foreign races and descent.' The bishops called for love of 'those innocent humans who are not of our people and blood.'"

Lewy also tells us that Cardinal Faulhaber, the highest-ranking Catholic clergyman in Germany at the time, said publicly in 1933 that there is nothing wrong with patriotism, and nothing wrong with racial pride, but that the Church forbids hatred of other nations, and teaches that one is not allowed to put loyalty to one's race above loyalty to the Church. "Faulhaber was severely criticized by the Nazis for these qualifications," Lewy says, "and his palace was fired upon." (Endnote 110.)

Obviously, the bishops did not think those statements violated the loyalty oath. Obviously, nothing in the Reichskonkordat stopped the bishops from teaching basic Christian ethics.

In 1941, Bishop Clemens von Galen denounced Hitler's policy of exterminating the mentally handicapped in a sermon to his congregation. Obviously Galen didn't think that was a disloyal statement. Obviously Galen didn't think that statement violated the Reichskonkordat.

Why does Posner not mention the times when the Catholic bishops spoke out against Hitler's policies? Because Posner has no desire to tell the whole truth, no desire to be fair.

Of course, the German bishops never encouraged Germans to revolt against Hitler, never said that would be a good idea. Criticize that if you want, but by the same token, when the German government started World War One for no good reason, and killed millions of enemy soldiers who were simply trying to defend their homelands, not one single rabbi in Germany objected. (I am sure that is true, because if any rabbi had objected, he surely would have been arrested, and quite possibly hanged for treason, and he would be famous today. He would be considered one of the great heroes of the twentieth century, on the same level as Martin Niemoller and Dietrich Bonhoeffer.) Look at Walter Isaacson's biography of Albert Einstein, or Albrecht Folsing's biography of Albert Einstein, and you will see that Einstein lived in Germany throughout World War One, and always told friends that he thought justice was not on Germany's side, that Germany had started the war for no good reason, and that he was hoping Germany would lose the war, but never did Einstein criticize the war effort publicly. If he had done that he would have been arrested, and perhaps hanged, and he certainly had no desire to take that risk. And when the British started the Boer War for no good reason, and forced Boer women and children into concentration camps where thousands of them died of malnutrition, did any rabbi in Great Britain denounce the war effort? Not that I ever heard, and surely if there had been such a rabbi, he would be famous today. So why does Posner rant on and on about how, in his opinion, the Catholic bishops should have said more, while simultaneously saying absolutely nothing about the times when rabbis, and Albert Einstein, were silent in the face of evil? Obviously, because Posner has no desire to be fair.

One has to remember, there was a widespread belief in the old days that during wartime, all good citizens must put aside their reservations and work for victory, and those who did not were scoundrels. That is why Woodrow Wilson, who certainly was not a stupid man, had Eugene Debs arrested and prosecuted during World War One for praising draft-dodgers. That is why Abraham Lincoln had Clement Vallandigham arrested and exiled during the Civil War. All Vallandigham was doing was saying the war was a tremendous waste of blood and treasure, and that the North had no right to impose its values on the South, but Old Abe wasn't going to tolerate that. He wasn't going to let Vallandigham run around the North giving anti-war speeches.

Eleventh, on page 91, Posner says Bishop Konrad von Preysing wanted the German bishops to issue a strong statement against the holocaust, but "His colleagues argued that the deportation of non-Catholics was troubling but not their duty to address. They refused to tell German Catholics that it was a mortal sin to kill Jews."

Posner is lying again. As I said just a few paragraphs ago, on pages 291 and 292 of his book *The Catholic Church and Nazi Germany*, the famous Jewish historian Guenter Lewy states that in August 1943, a joint pastoral letter of the German Catholic bishops "reminded the faithful that the killing of innocents was wrong even if done by the authorities and allegedly for the common good, as in the case of 'men of foreign races and descent.' The bishops called for love of 'those innocent humans who are not of our people and blood.'"

Twelfth, also on page 109, Posner tells us that "Catholics dominated the leadership of every puppet government allied with the Nazis." One feels amazed to read something that is so blatantly false. Does Posner really know nothing about World War Two? Norway in those days was a country with a minuscule Catholic population. Is Posner seriously trying to tell us that Catholics ran the puppet government there? Wikipedia says Vidkun Quisling, the Norwegian

Nazi leader, was raised as a Protestant, but in adulthood rejected Christianity and concocted his own private religion, which he called "universism." Wikipedia also says that Miklos Horthy, the Hungarian dictator who formed an alliance with Hitler, was a Protestant. Of course, as I have already said, Romania and Bulgaria were Eastern Orthodox countries with minuscule Catholic populations. Any good encyclopedia will tell you that, though Posner apparently is unaware of it. Finland was allied to Hitler, and was an overwhelmingly Protestant country, so I doubt very much that it was led by Catholics during the war. Croatia was led by a Nazi puppet who claimed to be a Catholic, but the leader of the Catholic Church in Croatia, Archbishop Alojzije Stepinac, repeatedly denounced the mass murders that the Croatian Nazis were committing. (Endnote 111.) In a speech that was broadcast on Vatican Radio, Stepinac said, "No temporal power, no political organization, has the right to persecute a man because of his race." (In those days, it was common to refer to every ethnic group as a "race." People would talk about the Irish race, the English race, the Jewish race, and so on.) How can you say the Croatian leaders were Catholics when they weren't willing to listen to their own archbishop? And Germany's Slovak client state had a president who claimed to be a Catholic, but look at page 485 of *The Years of Extermination: Nazi Germany and the Jews, 1939-1945* by the famous Jewish historian Saul Friedlander, and you will see that in September 1942, thousands of Jews were sent to Hitler's camps from Slovakia, but then the deportations stopped for a while. Then:

> "In the meantime rumors about the fate of the deportees had seeped back. Thus when Tuka [the Slovak prime minister] mentioned the possibility of resuming the deportations in early April 1943, protests from Slovak clergy, and also from the population, put an end to his initiative. On March 21,

a pastoral letter condemning any further deportations had been read in most churches."

Thirteenth, on page 86, Posner claims there were "vicious pogroms" in Poland in 1938 and 1939. HIs source of information for this claim is a book published in Germany in 1990. But a Jewish historian named Joseph Marcus has written an extremely detailed book called *Social and Political History of the Jews in Poland, 1919-1939*, and in that entire book, he never mentions any pogroms occurring in Poland in 1938 and 1939. Another Jewish historian named Martin Gilbert has written a book called *The Holocaust: A History of the Jews of Europe During the Second World War.* On page 51, Gilbert says that one day in 1936, a group of gentile hoodlums in Poland attacked some Jews and killed two of them. That is the only antisemitic violence in Poland that Gilbert mentions between January 1, 1930 and September 1, 1939. Surely if there had been "vicious pogroms" in Poland in 1938 and 1939, Gilbert would have mentioned them. A prominent historian named Norman Davies has written a book called *God's Playground: A History of Poland, Volume II, 1795 to the Present.* Davies says on page 426 that there was no "mass killing" of Jews in Poland in the 1930s until Hitler invaded. He certainly mentions no "vicious pogroms." A Jewish historian named David Kertzer wrote a book several years ago called *The Popes Against the Jews: The Vatican's Role in the Rise of Modern Anti-Semitism* in which he rants on and on about the horrible antisemitism that he thinks existed in the Catholic countries of Europe in the years prior to World War Two, but he never mentions any "vicious pogroms" in Poland prior to Hitler's invasion. I think therefore that Posner's claim that there were "vicious pogroms" in Poland in 1938 and 1939 is nonsense.

Fourteenth, on page 86, Posner quotes Cardinal Hlond, the highest ranking Catholic clergyman in Poland, as saying in a pastoral letter in 1936 "that the Jews are fighting against the Catholic Church, persisting in free thinking, and are the vanguard of godlessness, Bolshevism and subversion." That is the whole quote from Posner.

Hlond did indeed say those things, but he also said many other things in that pastoral letter, such as this: "I warn against that moral stance, imported from abroad, that is basically and ruthlessly anti-Jewish. It is contrary to Catholic ethics. One may not hate anyone. It is forbidden to assault, beat, maim or slander Jews. One should honor Jews as human beings and neighbors ... Beware of those who are inciting anti-Jewish violence. They serve an evil cause." (Endnote 112.)

Somehow Posner never finds time to mention that part of Hlond's pastoral letter.

Posner also fails to mention that after Hlond got done criticizing the Jews, he wrote, "But let us be fair. Not all Jews are this way." (Endnote 113.) Hlond went on to say that some Jews are "honest, just, kind and philanthropic." (Endnote 114.) Turning to economic matters, Hlond said, "It is good to prefer your own kind when shopping, to avoid Jewish stores ... but it is forbidden to demolish a Jewish store, damage their merchandise, break windows, or throw things at their homes." (Endnote 115.)

Fifteenth, on page 69. Posner says that when Mussolini invaded Ethiopia in 1936, Pope Pius XI "blessed some of the troops as they left for the fighting" in Ethiopia. His source of information for this is a book called *Worldly Goods*, published in 1971 by some guy named James Gollin. I don't believe that accusation, because if something this awful was true, surely it would be a well-known fact. Surely the militant atheists would mention it in their books, but they do no such thing. Page 5 of Michael Phayer's book *Pius XII, the Holocaust and the Cold War* says Mussolini asked Pius XI to bless the Italian troops as they headed off to Ethiopia, but Pius XI refused. Look at David Kertzer's book *The Pope and Mussolini: The Secret History of Pius XI and the Rise of Fascism in Europe*. Kertzer is certainly no friend of the Catholic Church. You can read about that in my book *David Kertzer Is Lying about Pope Pius XII.* But nowhere in *The Pope and Mussolini* does Kertzer say Pius XI ever blessed Italian troops who were on their way to fight in Ethiopia. Surely he would mention that, if it was true.

Sixteenth, On page 105, Posner claims Catholics were free to kill Jews, because Pius had "never issued a decree prohibiting their role in murdering Jews." That is simply not true. The church taught the Ten Commandments, and one of the Ten Commandments is "Thou shalt not commit murder." The church never said it was okay to violate that commandment if the victim was Jewish. I dare Posner to name one single time when any Catholic bishop said that. Even Martin Luther, an antisemite if there ever was one, never said that. Posner himself admits on page 96 that Pius, in his Christmas speech in 1943, lamented the fact that hundreds of thousands of people in Europe were being killed just because of their "nationality or race," but apparently by the time Posner got to page 105, he had forgotten what he had written on page 96.

The pope never specifically said it was a sin to kill soccer players either. Does that mean Catholics all over the world thought it was okay to kill soccer players? The pope never said it was a sin to kill Swedes, or left-handed people, or bartenders. Is Posner going to tell us that means Catholics all over the world thought it was okay to kill Swedes, left-handed people and bartenders?

It is a simple fact that before 1933, every country in Europe made it a crime to kill Jews, and the Vatican never complained about this, therefore anyone who wasn't a complete idiot knew that the Catholic Church considered it a sin to kill Jews.

What evidence does Posner have that any German Catholic thought it was not a sin to kill Jews? In all the trials that were held after the war ended, when did any defendant or witness say, "I am a Catholic and I thought it was okay to kill Jews" or anything like that? When did any witness say, "He killed Jews because he was a Catholic and he thought killing Jews wasn't a sin," or anything like that? I've never heard of anyone saying anything like that, and Posner certainly doesn't mention any such case.

Seventeenth, On page 66, Posner tells us "The Reichskonkordat convinced ordinary Germans that the Vatican approved of the Third Reich. German Catholics embraced the Nazis without any lingering reservations."

What evidence does Posner have to back up that claim? He doesn't say, obviously because he has no evidence. Does he seriously expect us to believe that someone was conducting public opinion polls among German Catholics in 1933 and asking if the church "approved of the Third Reich" and if they had any "lingering reservations"?

Even though John Cornwell dislikes Pius XII, he admits on page 147 of his book *Hitler's Pope* that in June 1933, thousands of members of the German Catholic Church's official political party, the Catholic Center Party, were arrested and jailed by the Nazis. Fritz Gerlich, a prominent Catholic newspaper editor and critic of the Nazis, was arrested, beaten to a pulp, and locked up in a concentration camp. That doesn't sound to me like Catholics in Germany were embracing the Nazi government "without any lingering reservations."

Eighteenth, on page 110, Posner writes, "Pius XII – when still a cardinal – had written and talked at length about how Jews were the masterminds of Russia's godless Bolshevik Revolution, and that their main goal was to destroy Christian civilization."

That is simply a lie. The only evidence Posner mentions in support of that ridiculous claim is a short passage that Pius wrote shortly after World War One, when he was not yet a cardinal. As a member of the Vatican diplomatic corps, he was sent to Germany to observe what was going on there. Germany was in severe turmoil at the time, and one day, Pius met with some revolutionaries who were trying to set up a communist government in Munich. In the report that he sent back to the Vatican, Pius mentioned that the leaders of the communist movement were mostly Jews, that the Jewish communist women had a "lecherous demeanor" and that the leader of the communist movement, whom Pius mistakenly thought was Jewish, was "vulgar and repulsive." (The leader's name was Max Levien. Pius and many other people thought that sounded like a Jewish name.) Nowhere did Pius say that all Jews are like that. He merely said Jewish communists that he met in Munich were like that. Nowhere does Posner mention any evidence that Pius thought or said or wrote that Jews were "masterminds of Russia's godless Bolshevik Revolution, and that their main goal was to destroy Christian civilization."

It is amazing that Posner would stoop to telling such a blatant lie. Pius's critics have looked over his record with a fine-tooth comb and have found no evidence, anywhere, that Pius thought Jews were "masterminds of Russia's godless Bolshevik Revolution, and that their main goal was to destroy Christian civilization."

It is perfectly obvious that Posner's goal is to deceive his readers, not educate them.

Ninteenth, on page 194, Posner says that in 1967, "The U.S. economy was growing at a robust 10 percent a year." That is nonsense. A financial news and advice website called TheBalance.com has a table of Gross Domestic Product growth in the United States for every year since 1929. The growth rate for 1966 was, oddly, 6.6 percent. In 1967 it was 2.7 percent. In 1968 it was 4.9 percent. I know from the economics course I took years ago that 10 percent is an extremely high rate of growth. Few countries have ever achieved it.

Twentieth, the *Miami New Times* is a muckraking and entertainment newspaper in Miami. In four issues, dated March 25, March 30, May 18, and May 20, all in the year 2010, articles by a journalist named Tim Elfrink said Posner is a plagiarist and is also in the habit of altering quotes from people. Wikipedia says Posner was "chief investigative reporter" for *The Daily Beast* website for a time, but after these four articles in the *Miami New Times* were published, he resigned in disgrace.

So, all in all, I don't think Posner's book can be taken seriously. Every nonfiction writer makes a mistake now and then, but Posner makes so many mistakes in *God's Bankers*, and some of them are such silly obvious mistakes, and he so often makes accusations that are backed up by no evidence whatever, that readers are left with no choice but to roll their eyes and throw his book in the trash. There is no way that we can have confidence that Posner has reported accurately about the complicated financial allegations that are the heart of his book.

ITEM 17: CONVENTIONAL WISDOM

A chap named Damon Linker reviewed Posner's book, *God's Bankers*, in the March 22, 2015 issue of the *New York Times Book Review*. Linker accused Pope Pius XI of "signing the Reichskonkordat with Hitler, which, in return for winning a measure of freedom for German Catholics under the Nazis, assured silence from the Holy See over the forced sterilization of 400,000 people and then only the faintest of objections to the Holocaust."

That is nonsense, except for the fact that in 1933, long before the war or the Holocaust started, Pius XI did indeed sign a treaty with Hitler, known in German as the Reichskonkordat. Posner's book doesn't say what Linker claims it says. As I explained earlier in this book, Pius XII's policy toward the Holocaust and other German atrocities was determined by his assessment that the Stalinists would be worse than the Nazis, and therefore it would be a blunder to undermine the Nazis. Pius also feared that if he denounced Hitler too vehemently, Hitler would retaliate against Catholics in some bloodthirsty way. The Reichskonkordat had nothing to do with it.

But anyone can see what is going on here. Pius XII's critics have spoken so often, and so loudly, that their negative portrayal of him has attained the status of conventional wisdom. People such as Damon Linker believe it even when they know almost nothing about the subject.

ITEM 18: SWEDEN'S IRON ORE

Forty percent of the iron ore that Hitler used during World War Two was sold to him by the socialist government of Sweden. (Endnote 116.) Hitler couldn't possibly have waged war without it. The socialists who ruled Sweden also allowed Nazi troops and equipment to travel through Sweden on their way to or from Nazi-occupied Norway, but did their best to keep out any German Jews who tried to flee to Sweden. (Endnote 117.) The Swedish socialists also censored the press during the war to prevent reports of Nazi atrocities from being published. It was feared that such reports might annoy Hitler and provoke him to invade Sweden. (Endnote 118.)

Isn't it interesting that the people who bash Pius XII night and day never complain about what the Swedish socialists did?

Of course, if you had asked the Swedish socialists why they were doing those things, I'm sure they would've said something like, "We haven't got a strong enough army to stand up to Hitler. If we refuse to sell iron ore to him, he'll invade Sweden, and a bunch of Swedes will get killed, and he'll get the iron ore anyway. So refusing to sell the ore to him won't do any good."

Precisely. And if you had asked the German Catholic bishops why they weren't publicly complaining about the mass murders that Hitler was committing against Jews, Poles, and other groups, they too would've said, "It'll just get us killed and it won't change a thing. The murders will keep happening anyway." In 1943, the German Catholic bishops published a public letter to the Catholics of Germany, saying that one must respect the right to life of all people, even "human beings of alien races and origin." (Endnote 118.) It seems to have had no impact whatever.

ITEM 19: JOHN CORNWELL AND HIS LIES

In 1999, a British journalist named John Cornwell published a biography of Pius XII called *Hitler's Pope*. The book is strange. Repeatedly, Cornwell tells us the facts, then draws conclusions that are not supported by the facts he has cited.

I am not the only one who finds the book unimpressive. It was reviewed in the September 27, 1999 issue of *Newsweek* magazine, and the reviewer, Kenneth L. Woodward, wrote that "errors of fact and ignorance of context appear on almost every page."

But let us examine the book in detail. All page numbers are from the hardcover edition.

On page 116, Cornwell admits that on October 11, 1930, the Vatican newspaper *L'Osservatore Romano* printed an editorial that said membership in the Nazi Party was "incompatible with the Catholic conscience."

On page 119, Cornwell admits that in the 1930 election, despite the Vatican's condemnation, the Nazis received 6.4 million votes, up from 800,000 in the previous election. This made the Nazis the second-largest party in Germany.

On page 109, Cornwell admits that the Catholic bishops of Bavaria issued a statement in 1931 saying Nazism was "incompatible with Catholic teaching." Later that year, the Catholic archbishops of Cologne and Paderborn said the same thing.

On page 110, Cornwell admits that in 1931, a German Catholic politician named Karl Trossman published a bestselling book called *Hitler and Rome*, in which he declared that the Nazis were "a brutal party that would do away with all the rights of the people," and that Hitler, if he ever got the chance, would start a war that would "end more disastrously than the last." Rarely in the history of politics has anyone made so accurate a prediction.

On pages 118-119, Cornwell admits that in 1930, Heinrich Bruning, a member of the Catholic Center Party, became chancellor of Germany. (The Germans call their prime minister the chancellor.) Bruning was a thoroughly decent chap, but he had no idea of what to do about the Great Depression. The conventional economists told him that he should cut government spending, so that is what he did, and it didn't work. He goes down in history as the German Herbert Hoover. Unemployment kept rising, and disgruntled blue-collar workers nicknamed him "the hunger chancellor."

On pages 126-127, Cornwell says that Bruning resigned in 1932, and the new chancellor called for new elections. The Nazis got 37.4 percent of the vote, more than any other party. The Catholic Center Party received only 16.2 percent. Cornwell admits that in addition to having the largest party, Hitler had a private army of 400,000 brownshirts and blackshirts, tough street-fighters who terrorized opposing parties and did anything Hitler told them to do. Cornwell also admits that after the election, the Catholic bishops of Germany publicly declared, once again, that Catholics were forbidden to belong to the Nazi Party, that high-ranking Nazis had made statements that were "hostile to the faith."

On pages 132-133, we read that Hitler became chancellor on January 30, 1933. In March 1933, new elections were held, and Hitler was able to form a coalition with a smaller right-wing party to get a majority. The Catholic Center Party received only 13.9 percent of the vote.

On pages 135-136, Cornwell admits that in 1933, Hitler asked the Reichstag to pass the Enabling Act, which allowed him to rule as a dictator. He needed two-thirds support to get it passed. Some in the Catholic Center Party opposed it, but after a stormy debate, the party's members in the Reichstag voted to support it, 60 to 14. Party chairman

Ludwig Kaas warned the fourteen that their lives would be in danger from Hitler's goons if they continued to oppose it. Former Chancellor Bruning opposed it, but then changed his mind, and persuaded the other thirteen to also change their minds, because he believed the Catholic Center Party needed unity so it could oppose any future government persecution. So the party supported it unanimously. It passed in the Reichstag by a vote of 441 to 94, so even if the Catholic Center Party had opposed it unanimously, it still would've passed.

On page 138, we read that in March 1933, the German Catholic bishops announced that from now on, Catholics could belong to the Nazi Party. Anyone can see what was happening here. The bishops had tried to prevent Hitler from coming to power, and had failed. Because of the Great Depression, the Nazis kept gaining popularity, and the Catholic Center Party kept losing popularity. Now the bishops were going to try co-operating with Hitler. (Of course, nobody foresaw at the time that Hitler would eventually commit genocide.) The bishops repeated publicly that they saw "religious-ethical errors" in Nazism, but said Catholics who opposed Hitler should not resort to illegal actions.

(Some may say the German Catholic bishops should have adamantly refused to co-operate with Hitler under any circumstances. If you think that way, you will have to condemn Harry Truman too, because, as I said earlier, Truman forged an alliance with the Spanish dictator Francisco Franco. Barack Obama, too, was willing to work with vicious thugs in order to win the war on terror. Look at his alliance with Prime Minister Narendra Modi of India, a mass murderer who instigated a pogrom that killed approximately two thousand Muslims in Gujarat in 2002. Endnote 120.)

On page 144, Cornwell admits that by mid-1933, the Catholic Center Party was in a state of "collapse," and was being abandoned by its supporters.

On pages 146-147, Cornwell admits that in June 1933, a "rally of Catholic apprentices" in Munich drew 25,000 participants, but it was broken up by Nazi thugs who beat up the Catholic apprentices, and chased them off the streets when they tried to hold a march and rally. Cardinal Faulhaber told his bishops to forbid all future rallies, "because we do not want to risk the lives of our young men and a government ban on youth organizations."

On page 147, Cornwell admits that in June 1933, thousands of Catholic Center Party members were arrested and jailed. Fritz Gerlich, a prominent Catholic newspaper editor and critic of the Nazis, was beaten to a pulp and locked up in a concentration camp.

Also on page 147, Cornwell calls the Catholic Church in Germany "mighty" but says it was in "a state of self-imposed inertia." He fails to say what he thinks it should have done.

Here we must stop and think. What on Earth is Cornwell babbling about? He admits on pages 126-127 that Hitler had a private army of 400,000 thugs who were ready and willing to kill at his command. What did the Catholic church have to counter that? Does Cornwell seriously think the church could've formed its own army of thugs and fought back against the Nazis? If it had tried to do that, Hitler would've surely found out about it, because something like that cannot be kept secret, and he would've arrested everyone involved in the effort. Is Cornwell really unable to see that his complaining is pointless unless he can explain what he thinks the church should've done?

Maybe Cornwell thinks the Catholic bishops could've ordered their followers, all over Germany, to march on Berlin and overthrow the government, much as Ayatollah Khomeini's followers overthrew the Shah of Iran in 1979. But Cornwell admits that in the 1933 election, the Catholic Center Party got only 13.9 percent of the vote. How can you seize power with only 13.9 percent of the people on your side, and many of them women and elderly men who would've been utterly useless in a street fight? When has any government, anywhere on the face of the Earth, been overthrown in that way?

Anyone can see what is going on here. Cornwell wants to blame Pius XII (who was merely Cardinal Pacelli, the Vatican secretary of state, at the time) and the Catholic bishops of Germany for the fact that Hitler seized power. He can't bear to face the obvious fact that they did everything they could to stop him, and nothing worked. Because of the Great Depression, the German people wanted the drastic medicine that Hitler was peddling. Bruning, the old-fashioned Catholic gentleman, had failed as chancellor. He and his party were thoroughly discredited. The Catholic bishops had denounced the Nazis repeatedly, but the Nazis became popular anyway. Cornwell insists that the Catholic bishops could've done something more to stop Hitler, but he never tells us what this something was. All he gives his readers is evasiveness.

The only force in Germany that could've thwarted Hitler and his 400,000 thugs was the army, and for some reason, the army didn't do it, even though there definitely were some generals who held Hitler in low regard. One suspects that the German generals saw that Hitler had a great deal of popular support, even among many army personnel, and believed trying to overthrow him would mean, basically, starting a civil war, and this they were unwilling to do.

Then Cornwell starts talking about the Concordat, the treaty between the Nazi government and the Vatican that was negotiated and signed in 1933, which specified what exactly the rights of the Catholic Church were going to be in Germany. On page 153, Cornwell claims that the Concordat "indicated ... Catholic moral approval of Hitler's policies." That is unmitigated hogwash. Cornwell himself admits on the same page that Pius XII, who was Cardinal Pacelli at the time and who was the chief negotiator of the Concordat, wrote in an article for the Vatican's official newspaper, shortly after the Concordat was negotiated, that signing the Concordat definitely did not mean the Vatican or the church approved of Hitler's policies. Cornwell also claims on page 153 that the Concordat "constrained the Holy See, the

German hierarchy, the clergy, and the faithful to silence on any issue the Nazi regime deemed political," and that the Concordat "had legally bound the Catholic Church in Germany to silence on outrages against the Jews." That too is nothing but a lie. Where in the Concordat did it say that? Cornwell never says, because he can't. The truth is that nothing in the Concordat said that. Cornwell himself mentions only Article 31, which stated that Catholic clergy could not join political parties or engage in "party political activity." Nothing in the Concordat said Catholic laypeople couldn't engage in politics or criticize the government, and nothing said the German bishops couldn't complain about government policies that they considered immoral. Cornwell never quotes any statements in the Concordat to that effect.

(For more information on this point, look at the book *The Catholic Church and Nazi Germany* by the prominent historian Guenter Lewy. That book talks quite a lot about the Concordat, but it never says the Concordat forbade Catholic bishops, priests or laypeople to criticize Hitler's policies. Lewy, who is Jewish, published that book in 1964, so it was available to Cornwell, if he had wanted to know the facts. Obviously, he did not want to know the facts.)

On page 157, Cornwell writes that the Concordat "imposed a moral duty on Catholics to obey the Nazi rulers. Thus Catholic critics fell silent." That is another barefaced lie. The Concordat imposed no such duty. Once again, Cornwell fails to quote any clause in the Concordat that had that meaning, because there was none. Apparently Cornwell can't bear to face the fact that if Hitler's "critics" in Germany "fell silent," it is because Hitler arrested them, or killed them, or thoroughly intimidated them. Cornwell himself admits on page 156 that Bruning, the former chancellor and leader of the Catholic Center Party, received so many death threats that he started sleeping in a different house every night, and then fled from Germany in 1934.

Why can't Cornwell see that violence and intimidation are almost always enough to make critics shut up?

On page 159, Cornwell admits that late in 1933, Cardinal Pacelli complained through diplomatic channels about the persecution of Catholic Jews in Germany. Cornwell admits that Hitler and his underlings refused to discuss the subject.

Then came the Blood Purge, June 30, 1934, when Hitler ordered his goons to arrest or kill many of his rivals and critics. At least eighty-five were killed, and perhaps far more than that. (We will never know for sure.) Cornwell admits on page 166 what I mentioned previously in this chapter: that four prominent Catholic laypeople, Erich Klausener, Fritz Gerlich, Adalbert Probst and Fritz Beck, were among those killed.

Cornwell doesn't mention this, but one can read in the Wikipedia article about Klausener that Klausener had recently spoken out publicly against the violence perpetrated by Hitler's goon squads, and about the fact that thousands of Germans were being held in prison without trial. If the Concordat forbid Catholic laypeople to criticize Hitler, as Cornwell claims, then why did Klausener, the head of the Catholic Action organization, say those things? The answer is obvious: the Concordat did not forbid Catholic laypeople to criticize Hitler's policies. Cornwell's claim that it did is a barefaced lie.

Cornwell also doesn't mention that shortly before the Blood Purge, a prominent Catholic politician named Franz von Papen delivered a speech in which he called for an end to "Nazi terror" and for restoration of freedom of the press. Klausener was one of the people who wrote that speech. (Endnote 121.) Once again we must ask, if Catholic laypeople were forbidden by the Concordat to criticize Hitler's policies, as Cornwell claims, why did von Papen deliver that speech?

Then Cornwell claims on page 166 that Cardinal Pacelli forbade the German Catholic bishops to complain about the murders of Klausener, Gerlich, Probst and Beck, but he presents no evidence to support this accusation. Apparently Cornwell thinks evidence is irrelevant. Does Cornwell think Pacelli sent a telegram to every German Catholic bishop, immediately after the murders happened, forbidding them to comment? He doesn't say. Did any German Catholic bishop ever say he would have publicly denounced the murders, but Cardinal Pacelli told him to not do it? Cornwell mentions no such bishop, and I have never heard of one. If you look at Guenter Lewy's famous book, *The Catholic Church and Nazi Germany*, you will see that Lewy never accuses Pacelli or Pope Pius XI of ordering the German Catholic bishops to stay silent about the murders. If it happened, why did Lewy not know about it?

Anyone with common sense can see that Cornwell, apparently, just can't bear to admit that the German Catholic bishops kept silent about these murders because it was obvious that complaints would only inflame Hitler's wrath and provoke more murders, and that nothing Cardinal Pacelli said or didn't say influenced them one bit.

On page 173, Cornwell admits that in 1935, Cardinal Pacelli publicly denounced the "superstition of race and blood" which had become popular in Germany. That, of course, was a denunciation of Nazism.

On pages 182 and 183, we read about Pope Pius XI issuing a letter to the German people, *Mit Brennender Sorge*, in 1937. The letter denounced Nazism and was read out loud in all Catholic churches in Germany during church services. Not surprisingly, Hitler became angry about this. Print shops that printed copies of the letter were shut down, and many employees were arrested. Hitler ordered all copies of it confiscated. Some messengers who delivered copies of it to parish priests avoided roads and walked through the woods instead, to avoid arrest.

On pages 193-196, Cornwell starts babbling about the Kulturkampf, an attempt by Otto von Bismarck's government in Germany in the 1800s to restrict the Catholic Church in various ways. He claims the Catholic Church could've stopped Hitler, because it stopped the Kulturkampf, eventually. On page 194, he writes, "Overall, the persecution during the Kulturkampf outstripped the persecution of the Catholic church by the Nazis between 1933 and 1938." That is simply not true. Cornwell himself has described Hitler's habit of murdering prominent Catholic laymen, while he doesn't mention one single Catholic clergyman or layman who was murdered during the Kulturkampf. Doesn't that prove, right there, that the persecution was worse under Hitler than during the Kulturkampf? Is Cornwell really unable to see something that is so obvious? Cornwell says eighteen hundred Catholic priests were jailed or expelled from Germany during the Kulturkampf. True enough, but thousands of clergymen and nuns were arrested by Hitler too. (Endnote 122.) On page 195, Cornwell says there was a lot of passive resistance to the Kulturkampf, and there could've been passive resistance to Hitler too, but there wasn't because of the "overwhelming influence in the 1930s of the Vatican policy of compliance." That strikes me as unlikely. After all, Hitler persecuted Protestants too, and one didn't see any passive resistance from them either. Cornwell says that during the Kulturkampf, German Catholics hid priests who were on the run from the authorities, and sometimes even broke into jails to free priests. True, but so what? No German Protestants broke into any jails when prominent Protestant clergymen such as Martin Niemoller and Dietrich Bonhoeffer were arrested.

Cornwell admits that Germany still had a free press and a parliament during the Kulturkampf, and of course did not during the Hitler years, and that may have made a difference. I'm sure it did. Cornwell also admits that Hitler had modern rapid communication and transportation, which Bismarck obviously did not have during the Kulturkampf, and that may have made a difference too. Again, I'm sure it did. But Cornwell fails to notice that Germany was simply a more religious country during the Kulturkampf than it was in the 1930s. Friedrich Nietzsche and his acolytes worked hard to turn Germany into a country of atheists, and they had considerable success. William L.

Shirer, an American journalist who covered Germany for CBS Radio News during the 1930s and early 1940s, has said that the average German was simply indifferent to the fact that the churches were being persecuted. The average German was more interested in the fact that Hitler had drastically reduced unemployment. (Endnote 123.)

Then on page 196, Cornwell starts talking about the so-called Rosenstrasse protest in Berlin in February 1943. The story he tells his readers is that the lives of two thousand Jewish men were saved because "hundreds" of their gentile wives spent a week demonstrating outside the building in which they were being held, chanting "Give us back our husbands!" and demanding that they be released.

It's a very uplifting story, but unfortunately it is fiction. The renowned historian Saul Friedlander discusses this incident on page 435 of his Pulitzer Prize-winning book *The Years of Extermination.* The Jews inside that building were never in any danger of being killed, Friedlander says. They had been summoned there only as a routine bureaucratic procedure, prior to being assigned to work at various places near Berlin, such as the only hospital in the region that still accepted Jewish patients. The number of "protesters" was never more than "a few score," and mostly they stood there silently, waiting for information, or else tried to smuggle food parcels into the building. This minor incident has been blown way out of proportion over the years, Friedlander says.

Of course, Friedlander's book was published several years after *Hitler's Pope* was, so maybe Cornwell sincerely believed the myth of the Rosenstrasse protests at the time when he was writing *Hitler's Pope.*

Because he believed this myth, Cornwell claims in *Hitler's Pope* that the Rosenstrasse protest is proof that civilian demonstrations could have ended the Holocaust, if only the Catholic and Protestant bishops had had the courage to start something like that. On pages 197-199 he argues that somehow Pius XII was responsible for the inaction of the German Catholic bishops. Obviously, his argument is rubbish. The

Rosenstrasse protest is a myth, and it is perfectly obvious that if any group had tried something like that in Nazi Germany, it would've been mowed down by a hailstorm of bullets. Just look at the fact that on page 162 of his book, *20th Century Journey: The Nightmare Years: 1930-1940*, William L. Shirer says that a few years before the war started, he knew two young German women who were arrested and beheaded just for making anti-Nazi statements at cocktail parties now and then.

On page 197, Cornwell claims that the Vatican "chose to repudiate" the Catholic Center Party. How? What did the Vatican do to harm the Catholic Center Party in any way? Cornwell doesn't say, obviously because he can't. He has no evidence whatever. He already admitted on page 147 that in 1933, Hitler had "thousands" of Catholic Center Party members arrested. Isn't it obvious that that is the reason why the party collapsed? People simply became afraid to be associated with it. That is not the fault of anyone in the Vatican.

On page 199, Cornwell claims Bishop Galen's complaints about Hitler's euthanasia program for the mentally ill are proof that protests against the Nazi regime could've been effective. But then, on the very same page, out of the other side of his mouth, he admits that despite Galen's complaints, the euthanasia program was "not entirely halted" and that there is reason to believe that Galen's criticism was "not crucial to the reduction of deaths."

One reads such stuff and shakes one's head in amazement. What is Cornwell thinking? He moves his queen forward on the chess board, then he immediately moves it back.

Also, on page 199, Cornwell writes, "Without the deadening hand of Vatican control, resistance might have been multiplied across the country from the outset." That is simply a lie. Pius XI and Pius XII did nothing to stop resistance. Cornwell presents not one single example of them doing that.

On page 280, Cornwell tells us "There were isolated but significant examples of Catholic bishops expressing anti-Semitic views even as the persecution of Jews gathered pace in Germany in the mid-1930s. In 1936, for example, Cardinal Hlond, primate of Poland, opined: 'There will be the Jewish problem as long as the Jews remain.'"

But Cornwall sees no need to mention that Hlond also said, in that same pastoral letter, "I warn against that moral stance, imported from abroad, that is basically and ruthlessly anti-Jewish. It is contrary to Catholic ethics. One may not hate anyone. It is forbidden to assault, beat, maim or slander Jews. One should honor Jews as human beings and neighbors ... Beware of those who are inciting anti-Jewish violence. They serve an evil cause." (Endnote 124.)

Hlond also said in that same pastoral letter that some Jews are "honest, just, kind and philanthropic." (Endnote 125.) But Cornwell doesn't mention that either.

When one looks at the facts that Cornwell omits, one can see that he has no desire to be honest.

On pages 296 and 297, Cornwell summarizes his case. He fails to consider the theory that I mentioned earlier, that has been put forward by Saul Friedlander and Michael Phayer: that Pius simply thought undermining Hitler would make things easier for Stalin, who was worse than Hitler. That explanation never occurs to Cornwell. Instead he concludes that Pius didn't want the Jews killed, but didn't care much about them either, that he felt "fear and distrust" of Jews, that this is why he was "not moved to pity and anger. From this point of view he was the ideal Pope (sic) for Hitler's unspeakable plan. He was Hitler's pawn. He was Hitler's Pope (sic)."

Those words have no connection to reality. As I have already pointed out, Pius's public denunciations of Hitler's policy of mass murder in Poland were also rare, so does that mean he felt "fear and distrust" of Poles too? Cornwell himself admits on pages 282 and 283 that when Hitler slaughtered 1,300 Czechs in reprisal for the murder, by the Czech underground, of a high-ranking Nazi official, Pius didn't publicly condemn that action either, so does that mean Pius felt "fear and distrust" of Czechs too? No, the explanation that best fits the evidence is that Pius feared that undermining Hitler would pave the way for Stalin to take over Germany and eastern Europe.

Next, on pages 304-306, Cornwell talks about the tragic incident on the morning of October 16, 1943, when the Nazis arrested approximately one thousand Roman Jews. Cornwell claims that at a meeting a few hours later, the German ambassador to the Vatican, Ernst von Weizsacker, told Cardinal Luigi Maglione, Pius's secretary of state, that the pope should publicly protest against these arrests. Cornwell has absolutely no evidence to support his claim that Weizsacker did this, and I know of no historian who agrees with him about this, though it certainly is true that Weizsacker was an old-fashioned Catholic aristocrat who was appalled by the Holocaust. Let me repeat what I said in Item 4: Michael Phayer discusses this incident in detail on pages 76 through 86 of his book, *Pius XII, the Holocaust, and the Cold War*. What happened at that meeting is that Cardinal Maglione vaguely threatened that if the Jews were not released, the pope would publicly denounce the arrests, which would be very embarrassing for the Germans. Weizsacker replied that if the pope did that, Hitler would surely find some grisly way to retaliate: there would be "consequences," he said. (Several months later, for example, when Italian rebels planted a bomb that killed a few German soldiers, the Germans retaliated by murdering 320 Italians, in what became known as the Ardeatine Caves massacre.)

Phayer tells us that next, Alois Hudal, a German bishop who was living in Rome at the time, sent a telegram to the German foreign minister, Joachim von Ribbentrop, urging an "immediate suspension of these arrests," and warning that the pope might publicly protest otherwise. Hudal signed the telegram, but Phayer doubts that he wrote it. Probably it was written by Weizsacker, he thinks, in league with some high-ranking Vatican officials. It is entirely possible that Pius himself wrote it. Then a few hours later, Weizsacker sent a telegram to Ribbentrop, saying pretty much the same thing that was in the Hudal telegram, and requesting that the arrested Jews be held in the vicinity of Rome for labor service instead of being sent to Auschwitz.

In the end, it was all for naught. The one thousand Roman Jews who had already been arrested were sent to Auschwitz, and almost all of them died there. Pius, apparently afraid of the "consequences" that Weizsacker had mentioned, made no public protest. But approximately six thousand other Jews were hidden in monasteries, convents, and other church buildings in Rome and its vicinity, which were not searched by the Germans, for fear that the pope would publicly protest if they were.

So the story is simple. In the face of German threats, Pius backed down. I don't see why anyone finds this shocking. German threats had to be taken seriously. As Pius surely knew, Hitler had proven repeatedly that he was willing to kill people for criticizing him.

On page 318 of *Hitler's Pope*, Cornwell quotes a Roman Jew who survived Auschwitz as complaining that Pius didn't warn the Jews of Rome that the arrests of October 16, 1943, were going to happen. That complaint makes no sense, because Cornwell presents no evidence that Pius knew the arrests were going to happen. Pius didn't find out about them until after they occurred. Cornwell also quotes that same Roman Jew as complaining that Pius "didn't take a single risk." That's right, he didn't, but I don't see why that is shocking. He didn't speak up on behalf of the thousand Roman Jews who were arrested and sent to Auschwitz because he could see that the Germans could easily retaliate by killing far more than a thousand people, if they so chose. Is anyone seriously going to argue that he shouldn't have been worried about that?

Dr. Joseph L. Lichten, an official of the Anti-Defamation League, wrote an essay about Pius XII in 1963, called "The Vatican & the Holocaust: A Question of Judgment – Pius XII & the Jews." You can read it at www.JewishVirtualLibrary.org[1]. (Click on "The Holocaust," then click on "The Vatican," then click on "Monograph on the Judgement of Pope Pius XII (1963)"). Lichten says he knew a German Jewish couple that managed to escape from Germany and ended up hiding in a convent in Italy. They said this to Lichten:

> "None of us wanted the Pope to take an open stand. We were all fugitives, and fugitives do not wish to be pointed at. The Gestapo would have become more excited and would have intensified its inquisitions. If the Pope had protested, Rome would have become the center of attention. It was better that the Pope said nothing. We all shared this opinion at the time, and this is still our conviction today."

Apparently Cornwell never heard of Lichten's essay.

---

1.   http://www.JewishVirtualLibrary.org/

ITEM 20: MARIA GORETTI

Cornwell also talks about Pius's activities after the war. On page 346 of *Hitler's Pope*, he mentions Saint Maria Goretti, an Italian girl from a peasant family who, in 1902, was repeatedly propositioned for sex by a young man. She kept saying no to him. He kept threatening to kill her if she didn't give in. Finally, one day, he stabbed her to death. It is important to remember that, according to what I read years ago, no rape or attempted rape occurred. He just stood there with his knife, and demanded that she give in, and she said no once again, and so he stabbed her. Obviously, she was very brave, and Pius XII admired her and declared her a saint in 1950. Cornwell asks, why did Pius say Catholics had no duty to risk their lives to save Jews, but did have a duty to risk their lives to avoid being raped? The answer is that Pius did not say that people have a duty to risk their lives to avoid being raped. Cornwell fails to see that praising Maria Goretti for being brave is not the same thing as saying that all Catholics have an obligation to act the same way she did. Similarly, Pius praised the Catholics who were brave enough to stand up to Hitler, such as Bishop Galen, but he never said every Catholic had an obligation to be that brave. Similarly, Pius doubtless would've said that it is very admirable, even saintly, for a rich man to give away all his money and become a monk, but he never said every rich Catholic had an obligation to do that. No pope has ever said that it is sinful to not be perfect.

I'm afraid one must conclude that Cornwell either repeatedly fails to understand the facts that he reports, or else is a cynic who decided he could make more money by writing a book bashing Pius XII than by writing an honest book.

CONCLUSION

It is certainly possible the Pius made mistakes here and there, as all leaders do. Maybe he should've taken more risks. Maybe he should've been more eager to embrace martyrdom. But this notion, peddled by Daniel J. Goldhagen, John Cornwell and others, that Pius could've done a great deal more to help Jews, but refused out of callousness, has no foundation in fact. The simple fact is he was more afraid of Stalin than of Hitler, and he had good reasons for being more afraid of Stalin than of Hitler, and therefore he believed undermining Hitler would help Stalin and would be disastrous for European civilization. Therefore, once Hitler invaded the Soviet Union, Pius was not going to undermine Hitler. As far as the Jews are concerned, Pius was not going to risk getting a hundred thousand more Polish, Czech, Dutch, Belgian and French Catholics killed just to save a few thousand Jews. Pius's critics never explain why they think he should have done that. Obviously, they have no explanation, and they just aren't honest enough to admit it.

ENDNOTES

1. See page 570 of the book *The Years of Extermination: Nazi Germany and the Jews, 1939-1945*, by Saul Friedlander, a book which won a Pulitzer Prize.

2. Ibid, pages 569-573.

3. Ibid, page 620.

4. For the facts in this paragraph, see pages 22-27 of Michael Phayer's book *The Catholic Church and the Holocaust, 1930-1965*. Phayer was a history professor at Marquette University, and I think Goldhagen will admit that Phayer is a reliable source of information, because Goldhagen himself, in *A Moral Reckoning*, uses him as a source.

5. For the facts in this paragraph, see pages 149-156 of William L. Shirer's book, *20th Century Journey: The Nightmare Years, 1930-1940*. Shirer was a well-regarded American journalist who covered Europe in the 1930s for CBS Radio News.

6. See page 513 of *The Years of Extermination* by Saul Friedlander. There is also an article about Sophie Scholl in Wikipedia.

7. See pages 269-270 of the book, *The Wages of Guilt: Memories of War in Germany and Japan* by the prominent journalist Ian Buruma.

8. See page 202 of Saul Friedlander's book, *The Years of Extermination*.

9. Ibid.

10. See page 156 of William L. Shirer's book, *20th Century Journey: The Nightmare Years, 1930-1940*.

11. See page 516 of *The Years of Extermination* by Saul Friedlander.

12. See page 53 of Michael Phayer's book, *Pius XII, the Holocaust and the Cold War*.

13. See a review by John Gray in the November 25, 2013 issue of *New Republic* magazine.

14. See page 535 of *The Years of Extermination* by Saul Friedlander.

15. See pages 374-375 of the second edition of the book, *Anne Frank: The Biography*, by Melissa Muller, published in 2013.

16. See pages 576-577 of *The Years of Extermination* by Saul Friedlander.

17. See the Wikipedia article about Lidice. You can also read about Lidice massacre on pages 991 thru 993 of *The Rise and Fall of the Third Reich* by William L. Shirer, or you can watch a film about Lidice at the U.S. Holocaust Memorial Museum.

18. See page 406 of *Bloodlands: Europe Between Hitler and Stalin* by Timothy Snyder.

19. You can read an article about Corrie Ten Boom in Wikipedia. The name of her book is *The Hiding Place*.

20. See pages 282-283 of David S. Wyman's critically-acclaimed book, *The Abandonment of the Jews: America and the Holocaust, 1941-1945*.

21. See pages 565-568 of *The Years of Extermination* by Saul Friedlander.

22. See pages 234-240 of John Cornwell's book *Hitler's Pope*, and page 43 of Daniel J. Goldhagen's book, *A Moral Reckoning*.)

23. See page 178 of *Pius XII, the Holocaust and the Cold War* by Michael Phayer.

24. See page 284 of *Hitler's Pope* by John Cornwell.

25. See page 415 of Timothy Snyder's critically-acclaimed book *Bloodlands: Europe Between Hitler and Stalin*, or read reviews of that book in the November 11, 2010 issue of the *New York Review of Books* and the November 28, 2010 issue of the *New York Times Book Review*.

26. See pages xiv and 415 of *Bloodlands* by Timothy Snyder.

27. Ibid, page x.

28. See the article by Richard Pipes in the November 20, 2014 issue of the *New York Review of Books*.)

29. See pages 225-226 of the book, *The Spanish Revolution* by the highly-regarded history professor Stanley G. Payne.

30. See page 46 of *The Years of Extermination* by Saul Friedlander.

31. See page 318 of *Bloodlands* by Timothy Snyder.

32. See pages 39 and 40 of *The System: An Insider's Life in Soviet Politics*, by Georgi Arbatov.

33. See pages 55-66 of Michael Phayer's book, *The Catholic Church and the Holocaust, 1930-1965*.

34. See pages 76-86 of Michael Phayer's book, *Pius XII, the Holocaust, and the Cold War*.

35. See page 217 of John McCain's book *Worth the Fighting For.*

36. See pages 356-357 in *The Collected Essays, Journalism and Letters of George Orwell: An Age Like This: 1920-1940*, edited by Sonia Orwell and Ian Angus.

37. Ibid, pages 394-398.

38. See page 457 in Ronald W. Clark's book *The Life of Bertrand Russell.*

39. Ibid, pages 460-461.

40. See page 56 of Michael Phayer's book *The Catholic Church and the Holocaust, 1930-1965*.

41. See page 406 of *Bloodlands* by Timothy Snyder.

42. See page 24 of Michael Phayer's book *The Catholic Church and the Holocaust, 1930-1965*. Also, the entire text of *Summi Pontificatus* can be found on the Internet.

43. See page 25 of Michael Phayer's book, *The Catholic Church and the Holocaust, 1930-1965*.

44. Ibid.

45. See page 568 of *The Years of Extermination* by Saul Friedlander.

46. See page 26 of Michael Phayer's book, *The Catholic Church and the Holocaust, 1930-1965*.

47. Ibid, page 27.

48. Ibid, page 26.

49. Ibid, page 23.

50. Ibid, page 61.

51. See page 570 of *The Years of Extermination: Nazi Germany and the Jews, 1939-1945*, by Saul Friedlander.

52. See page 27 of *The Catholic Church and the Holocaust, 1930-1965* by Michael Phayer.

53. See pages 124 and 169-171 of the book *The Catholic Church and Nazi Germany*, by the famous historian Guenter Lewy.

54. Ibid, page 124.

55. Ibid, pages 169-174.

56. See page 279 of *The Rise and Fall of the Third Reich* by William L. Shirer.

57. See page 124 of *The Catholic Church and Nazi Germany* by Guenter Lewy.

58. Ibid, pages 130-150.

59. See page 43 of the book *The Holocaust* by Martin Gilbert.

60. See an article by Philip Taubman in the July 21, 1983 issue of the *New York Times*, and an article by Alan Riding in the January 23, 1983 issue of the *New York Times*, and an opinion piece by an Israeli human rights activist named Benjamin Beit-Hallahmi in the January 6, 1983 issue of the *New York Times*, and an article by Leslie Gelb in the December 17, 1982 issue of that same newspaper.

61. See page 18 of *Nuremberg: Infamy on Trial*, by Joseph E. Persico.

62. Ibid, page 438.

63. See pages 355, 361, and 393-395 of the book *A People Betrayed: A History of Corruption, Political Incompetence and Social Division in Modern Spain* by Paul Preston.

64. See pages 275-277, 285, and 291 of *The Wages of Guilt: Memories of War in Germany and Japan*, by the highly-regarded journalist Ian Buruma.

65. See pages 160-165 of *Pius XII, the Holocaust, and the Cold War*, by Michael Phayer.

66. These polls are reported on pages 57-58 of the book *Postwar: A History of Europe Since 1945*, by the famous history professor Tony Judt.

67. See page 268 of *Pius XII, the Holocaust, and the Cold War*, by Michael Phayer.

68. See pages 159-163, 176-179, 235-236, and 475-476 of *Von Braun: Dreamer of Space, Engineer of War*, by Michael J. Neufeld.

69. Ibid, page 472.

70. See the article about Strughold by Anjana Ahuja in the April 2, 2001, issue of *The Times* of London.

71. See the article by George Lardner in the April 28, 2001, issue of the *Washington Post*. For an overview of the entire program of covering up the crimes of Nazi scientists and other Nazis so they would help the anti-communist West, see Linda Hunt's book, *Secret Agenda: The United States Government, Nazi Scientists, and Project Paperclip, 1945-1980*.

72. See page 440 of Joseph Persico's book *Nuremberg: Infamy on Trial*.

73. See pages 228-230 and 235-238 of *Pius XII, the Holocaust, and the Cold War*, by Michael Phayer, and pages 173-174 of *The Catholic Church and the Holocaust, 1930-1965*, by the same author.

74. See David K. Shipler's article in the February 9, 1983, issue of the *New York Times*.

75. See an article called "Excerpts from Report on Israel's Responsibility in Massacre," in the February 9, 1983 issue of the *New York Times*.

76. See page 44 of a book by Amos Oz called *The Slopes of Lebanon*, translated by Maurie Goldberg-Bartura.

77. See pages 162-163 of Thomas Friedman's book, *From Beirut to Jerusalem*.

78. See an editorial called "Judgment in Jerusalem," on pages 9 through 12 of the March 7, 1983, issue of *New Republic* magazine.

79. See page 290 of *The Collected Essays, Journalism and Letters of George Orwell: My Country Right or Left, 1940-1943*, edited by Ian Angus and Sonia Orwell, and page 339 of *The Collected Essays, Journalism and Letters of George Orwell: As I Please, 1943-1945*, edited by Ian Angus and Sonia Orwell.

80. See page 110 of *A Lethal Obsession: Anti-Semitism from Antiquity to the Global Jihad*, by a prominent Jewish history professor named Robert S. Wistrich.

81. Ibid, page 111.

82. See pages 43-53 of *Antisemitism: The Longest Hatred* by Robert S. Wistrich.

83. Go to the index of Richard Dawkins's book *The God Delusion*. Look up H.G. Wells and go to that page. I doubt Dawkins would say something so horrible about a fellow atheist if it wasn't true.

84. See an article by Kwame Anthony Appiah in the May 9, 2019 *New York Review of Books*.

85. See page 93 of William L. Shirer's book, *The Collapse of the Third Republic*.

86. See page 225 of *Mencken: A Life*, by Fred Hobson.

87. Ibid, page 423.

88. See page 286 of Mencken's book *Treatise on the Gods*, second edition.

89. See page 333 of *The Collected Essays, Journalism and Letters of George Orwell: As I Please, 1943-1945*, edited by Sonia Orwell and Ian Angus.

90. See pages 377-378 of *The Collected Essays, Journalism and Letters of George Orwell: My Country Right or Left, 1940-1943*, edited by Sonia Orwell and Ian Angus.

91. Ibid, pages 290-291.

92. See an article about Nemirovsky in the January 30, 2008 issue of *New Republic* magazine.

93. See pages 144 and 145 of *Henry Ford and the Jews: The Mass Production of Hate* by Neil Baldwin.

94. Ibid, pages 172 and 173.

95. Ibid, pages 283 thru 285.

96. See page 53 of *Antisemitism: The Longest Hatred*, by Robert Wistrich.

97. See page 376 of *The Collected Essays, Journalism and Letters of George Orwell: As I Please, 1943-1945*, edited by Sonia Orwell and Ian Angus.

98. The fact that Trotsky, Kamenev and Zinoviev were in the politburo is on page 464 of Ronald W. Clark's book, *Lenin: A Biography*. The fact that they were Jews is on page 160 of Robert S. Wistrich's book, *A Lethal Obsession: Anti-Semitism from Antiquity to the Global Jihad*.

99. See page 249 of Saul Friedlander's book, *The Years of Extermination: Nazi Germany and the Jews, 1939-1945*.

100. See pages 31 and 290 of the book *Social and Political History of the Jews in Poland, 1919-1939*, by Joseph Marcus.

101. See pages 448 and 449 of Paul Johnson's book, *A History of the Jews*.

102. See Walter Isaacson's article in the December 2009 issue of the *Atlantic Monthly*, page 72.

103. Look at the Wikipedia article, "1891 New Orleans Lynchings," and the book *The 1891 New Orleans Lynching and U.S.-Italian Relations: A Look Back*, by Marco Rimanelli and Sheryl Lynn Postman.

104. See pages 398 and 399 of *The Last Million: Europe's Displaced Persons from World War to Cold War*, by David Nasaw.

105. See pages 10 and 11 of *Einstein: The Life and Times*, by Ronald W. Clark.

106. See page 25 of Michael Phayer's book, *The Catholic Church and the Holocaust, 1930-1965*.

107. You can find these facts in the Wikipedia article called "Italian Republic (Napoleonic.)"

108. See pages 261 and 265-266 of Alan Brinkley's book, *Voices of Protest: Huey Long, Father Coughlin, and the Great Depression.*

109. Ibid, pages 265 and 266.

110. See page 131 of *Betrayal: German Churches and the Holocaust,* edited by Robert P. Ericksen and Susannah Heschel.

111. See pages 12 thru 14 of *Pius XII, the Holocaust and the Cold War,* by Michael Phayer.

112. See pages 271-272 of *Constantine's Sword,* by James Carroll.

113. See page 26 of *The Years of Extermination: Nazi Germany and the Jews, 1939-1945,* by Saul Friedlander.

114. See page 98 of Robert S. Wistrich's book, *A Lethal Obsession: Anti-Semitism from Antiquity to the Global Jihad.*

115. See Page 275-276 of *The Popes Against the Jews* by David Kertzer.

116. See pages 83 and 84 of *Postwar: A History of Europe Since 1945* by the famous history professor Tony Judt.

117. See pages 107 and 116-117 of the book *Raoul Wallenberg: The Biography,* by Ingrid Carlberg.

118. Ibid, pages 138 and 139.

119. See page 516 of *The Years of Extermination: Nazi Germany and the Jews, 1939-1945,* by Saul Friedlander.

120. You can read about Modi's pogrom in an article by Barry Bearak in the April 5, 2002 *New York Times,* and you can read about Obama's alliance with him in an article by Gardiner Harris and Coral Davenport in the June 8, 2016 issue of the same newspaper, and in an editorial in the June 14, 2016 issue of the same newspaper.

121. See page 218 of *The Rise and Fall of the Third Reich* by William L. Shirer.

122. See page 156 of William L. Shirer's book, *20th Century Journey: The Nightmare Years, 1930-1940,* and see an article by the

prominent historian Istvan Deak in the November 5, 2001 issue of *New Republic* magazine.

123. See page 156 of William L. Shirer's book, *20th Century Journey: The Nightmare Years, 1930-1940.*

124. See pages 271-272 of *Constantine's Sword: The Church and the Jews – A History*, by James Carroll.

125. See page 98 of Robert S. Wistrich's book, *A Lethal Obsession: Anti-Semitism from Antiquity to the Global Jihad.*

THE END

If you enjoyed this book, perhaps you will also enjoy these other books by the same author:

Darwin Wanted to Exterminate the Blacks, and Other Facts About Famous Atheists

David Kertzer Is Lying About Pope Pius XII

Richard Dawkins Lies Like a Rug

Christopher Hitchens Lied Like a Rug

Carl Sagan Lied Like a Rug

Sam Harris Lies Like a Rug

Enlightenment How? The Lies and Evasions of Steven Pinker

John F. Kennedy Stole the 1960 Presidential Election

Israel's Genocide in Guatemala

Michelle Obama Doesn't Know What She's Talking About

Nicholas Kristof Doesn't Know What He's Talking About

Are There Ghosts in the White House?

Gloria Steinem and Her Lies

Edward O. Wilson: The Man Who Sneered at Morality

Christianity Has a Better Moral Record than Atheism

Hitler Hated Christianity

Evolution Favors People Who Don't Believe in Evolution

Liberals Should Like the Electoral College